Love's Not Color Blind

Love's Not Color Blind

Race and Representation in Polyamorous and Other Alternative Communities

by Kevin A. Patterson, M.Ed.
with a foreword by Ruby Bouie Johnson

THORNAPPLE PRESS

Thornapple Press
300–722 Cormorant Street
Victoria, BC V8W 1P8 Canada
press@thornapplepress.com

Thornapple Press (formerly Thorntree Press) is a brand
of Talk Science to Me Communications Inc. Our business
offices are located in the traditional, ancestral and unceded
territories of the lək‌ʷəŋən and ẉsÁNEĆ peoples.

Cover design by Wolf McFarlane and Franklin Veaux
Interior design by Jeff Werner
Editing by Tonya Martin
Proofreading by Roma Ilnyckyj
Indexing by Catherine Plear

Library of Congress Cataloging-In-Publication Data
is available for this title.

10 9 8 7 6 5 4 3

Printed in the United States of America on acid-free
paper that is certified by the Forest Stewardship
Council and the Rainforest Alliance.

*This book is dedicated
to my children. All I can teach you
is how to freely be yourselves.
From what I've seen of you,
that should be enough.*

CONTENTS

FOREWORD

I met Kevin Patterson's reputation before I met Kevin Patterson the person. Others described Kevin as an amazing leader and powerful force of nature. In the six to nine months that preceded our official introduction, I was peppered with:

"Do you know Kevin Patterson?"

"Have you talked to Kevin Patterson?"

"You need to talk to Kevin Patterson."

Over the course of those months, my activism, involvement, and criticisms of the polyamorous community became well known. As a black woman, my criticisms and concerns are similar to those that Kevin discusses in his pioneering inaugural book, *Love's Not Color Blind*. The more vocal I became about my concerns, the more assertive folks became about me speaking with Mr. Patterson.

As I write this foreword, I recall my initial thoughts of the insistence that I meet Kevin. Though Kevin and I are active in the polyamorous communities, personally, my focus is therapy and education. So, I was perplexed, yet intrigued by where and how we could connect. My first meaningful interaction came about as the result of a colleague recommending that I complete an interview for *Poly Role Models*. Unbeknownst to me, Kevin founded and curates *Poly Role Models*. The interview consisted of me answering questions about my journey and my experience as a black polyamorous person. Briefly, I was introduced to polyamory in 2012. Since 2012, my relationship with myself and my relationships with others have become more rich and intimate. I embrace vulnerability, which liberates me from who others believe I am and gives me the freedom to be who I am. My newfound liberation gave me the courage to start my practice. In 2014, I opened my private practice as a sex therapist in Plano, Texas. In 2015, I founded

PolyDallas Millennium LLC, which is an annual symposium held in Dallas that educates and celebrates the various relationship styles. With intentionality, we uplift the voices for people of color.

Over the course of the last few years, I have witnessed leaders pushing for the need to have intentional spaces for black folks in diverse relationship styles to ask questions and to have open conversations about the unique needs of black Americans. To be noted, these conversations are not new. Pioneers, such as Ron Young, Michón Neal, Kato Cooks, Aida Manduley, Dirty Lola, and many others, have kept the conversations going until folks like Kevin that have the passion create their platform. In my experience, leaders leave different markers of their legacy based upon their strengths. Some are creative with their ideas. Some are writers and public figureheads. Some are like Kevin and have the ability to reach many different groups and code switch on a dime. He reminds me of President Barack Obama's famous code switch captured on video and viewed by millions of fans. Let's right size this comparison slightly—our President has a bit more swag. Kevin's about two miles behind in the swag area. He is catching up, though.

I met Kevin at Loving More in Philadelphia. He attended with his gorgeous wife, Autumn. I felt his sincerity and genuineness from the first moment I met him. My relationship with Kevin followed the trajectory of professional colleague, to mentor, and landed as a friend. I knew he had been speaking and putting out *Poly Role Models* for some time. When I submitted my story, he informed me that I would not be out for about three months. My thoughts were "Damn, big balla." I am honored to be on the list. Kevin and I clicked from the very beginning. I called him out of the blue because I was feeling anxious and uncertain. I needed a lot of validation, and Kevin was patient and supported me. He was always humble and stated that he did not have all the answers. However,

Kevin, Chris Smith, and I made a commitment to hold each other accountable.

I believe what connects us is the shared narrative of our experiences. *Love's Not Color Blind* recounts his personal experiences and other's experiences about being black, women, queer, sex workers, who are well known in the communities. Throughout the book, Kevin shares relevant and timely experiences of himself and others. Showcasing these voices does not happen. A book about the polyamorous written by a black man has just happened in 2017. This is a historical moment. Kevin and I are a part of many social media groups and email lists. Those lists discuss "inclusivity" and how can we diversify the polyamorous community. Even though the polyamorous community espouses connection and community, sometimes we fall short. We don't realize how short we are falling. *Love's Not Color Blind* exposes the imposter syndrome within our community. We present with a strong face and strong words, but there is an afraid and insecure community that does not want to be found out.

I am an educator, writer, blogger, and symposium organizer. I am an avid reader. With intention, I seek the black voice within all areas. As a sex educator, it's not a secret that there are not enough black voices. This is glaringly evident within the polyamorous field. There are many "how-to books" that are psychoeducational. From the beginning, Kevin informs the reader that *Love's Not Color Blind* is not a "how-to book." This book is written by a black man and speaks to black people. Black people have been spectators to the white experience long enough. Kevin fills a much-needed gap in the literature within the polyamorous community.

Love's Not Color Blind takes the reader on an amazing journey that is hearty and fulfilling. Through an amazing conversational tone that invites the reader to the dinner table, Kevin serves the reader a plate of soul food. Kevin's anecdotal experiences are like a side of the ham hock and greens. Those greens are seasoned perfectly with 15 years of experience in the polyamorous communities and a vaster vantage point as a result of being a service leader. Like a skilled cook, Kevin complements his experiences with the voices of community members, leaders, and advocates. Like a mound of cheesy and artery-clogging mac and cheese, those voices are decadent and rich. *Love's Not Color Blind* is not only a book full of community narratives. Kevin cites research articles, political figures, comic book heroes, theorists, and educators. The dessert is a piece of pecan pie that is his sweet charm, wit, and uncanny ability to bring it all together. When you leave the table, you are satisfied and say, "Damn, that was some good shit."

Love's Not Color Blind by Kevin Patterson is finally here. I am beyond honored and floored to write the foreword to this book. I am proud of you, my brother. I want to leave you with the famous words of another leader, Shaft (1971). Bumpy Jonas: "When will I hear from you?" John Shaft: "When I got something to say."

Kevin Patterson, I hear you loud and clear.

– Ruby B. Johnson LCSW, LCDC
Sex Therapist, Sexuality Educator, Blogger, and Writer
CEO and Organizer of PolyDallas
Millennium LLC's Annual Symposium

ACKNOWLEDGMENTS

This book was written under the emotional influence of the strongest group of women who have ever wasted their time loving a jerk like me.

This book was written under the stabilizing influence of the snarkiest bunch of assholes who I've ever had the good fortune to call my closest friends.

This book was written under the artistic influence of Nas, Kendrick Lamar, De La Soul, Ghostface Killah, Talib Kweli, Common, and The Roots....

Thank you.

Beginning Stuff...

I use a lot of analogies.

But before I get into all that, I'd like to mention that I am a cisgender, heterosexual, well-educated, (maybe upper-) middle class, able-bodied, tall, attractive, black man. I am packed with privileges in American society, which is the society under which I've lived my entire life. In regards to those privileges, I understand that I'm never going to have to worry about a reference to my spouse or romantic partners leading to my firing.

I don't ever have to worry about which bathroom I plan to use, at the risk of my safety or freedom.

I never have to pay attention to the location of curb cuts as I approach a crosswalk.

I try to remain cognizant of these privileges, and I work to destabilize the systems that put them in place...that keep them in place. If I make any mistakes along the way, I ask that you please make me aware. If you've got the time, the means, and the mental energy to spare, I welcome the upgrade.

Of all the self-identities I mentioned earlier, the one in which I am *not* privileged, is my race.

I *do* have to worry about whether my skin color will be a factor when I'm sitting across from an employer, or a loan officer, or a real estate agent. I'm a person of color. Race is the place through which I filter my understanding of all marginalized people.

And that's why I make analogies.

It's been my experience that the marginalization of people of color in American society often mirrors the marginalization of women...and queer folks...and trans people, etc. Educators have a concept called the "Zone Of Proximal Development" or ZPD. Introduced by Russian psychologist Lev Vygotsky, ZPD is the idea of recognizing the difference between what a learner can figure out on their own and what they might need help to accomplish. For me, that zone was in seeing the oppression of others through my own lens. I understood the struggles of people of color, but I needed some unexpected help when it came to understanding what women and others go through.

My personal acceptance of intersectional feminism came from listening to a woman describe her experiences with misogyny and rape culture, and observing a man entering the discussion and attempting to invalidate what she had gone through.

Everything that this man said sounded so similar to what I've heard white people say when I describe my own experiences with racism and police overreach. Not the *exact* words, but definitely identical context and tone. This man used the same circular logic, the same dismissive attitude, the same clueless rationalizations stemming from a lack of lived experience with the topic at hand…And I was left with the same feeling that, after this discussion, that smug asshole would write-off everything this woman had told him — because he could — and because he'd never have to think about it in the context of his personal safety versus a societal construct that he couldn't change.

Up to that point, I could've been (and probably was) "that guy." After that point, I realized that I had been as dismissive to women, their autonomy, and their shared experience with oppression as others had been towards me.

I was a part of the problem.

So, from that point, I spent more time listening and less time debating when it came to experiences for which I had no personal reference. It's through my own life, dealing with racism, that I try to relate and empathize with the troubles that other identities are faced with. I try to reflect this when I speak, and I try to do the same when I write.

Obviously, analogies aren't perfect. If they were perfect, you wouldn't have an analogy. You'd just have the thing the analogy is referencing, and that would stand on its own. But as these topics often require deeper explanation, analogies are us.

What I ask is that you don't get too lost in the weeds.

If I reference "racism and transphobia," I hope you understand that I'm not saying that the lives and experiences of people of color are a one-to-one comparison with that of transgender people. They aren't, and I'd be silly to say so. What I'm (likely) saying is that these people suffer from similar concerns at the hands of similar oppressive factors.

If you decide to track each analogy all the way back to their respective breaking points ****spoiler alert**** you'll end up having to remove ALL shared culture and ALL social context. You'll be left with only individuals.

Every single individual on the planet has a unique personal experience. At that point, you might as well not have this book or any non-fiction book about any sociological topic because "your mileage may vary" equally applies to everyone.

That would be boring as fuck, wouldn't it?

Is that what you want? Probably not. For your benefit and mine, let the analogies be their own wonderfully imperfect selves.

DISCLAIMER 2: ELECTRIC BOOGALOO…

An analogy (surprise!): Dana and Rose, in two separate bathroom shower occurrences, accidently kick the edge of their respective bathtubs. Dana stubs her toe and is left in a lot of pain. Rose breaks her foot.

Although she is in pain, Dana is able to walk, get dressed, and continue with life just fine…with the exception of a slight limp that she'll have for another hour or so. She goes to work that day and complains about her foot to any coworker who will listen.

Through all of this, Rose's life has been severely impacted. Rose can't drive her car with a broken foot. She will need help, either by ambulance or friendly neighbor, to reach the hospital. Once there, she will need to have surgery on that broken foot. After the surgery heals, Rose will have to undergo weeks of physical therapy to be able to walk properly again. All of this means days off of work, leading to late payments on her bills, a series of missed social events, a logistically altered sex life, etc. As a result of one event, kicking the bathtub, Rose's life experienced a major turn.

Now imagine if Dana and Rose were in the same social circle discussing their respective injuries. Imagine if, whenever Rose talked about her broken foot, Dana talked over her: "Really? I hurt my foot, too, and I was back to work the same day. I kicked the edge of the bathtub, just like you did. I don't know why you needed surgery or physical therapy. *I* didn't. In fact, we should both have equal access to those resources due to our similar foot injuries."

Their situations aren't the same, but Dana demanded that they be — for the sake of debate — in this conversation. When the conversation is over, Dana won't think about her stubbed toe until the topic comes up in conversation again. Her foot was back to normal before noon on the day that she hurt it.

Rose, on the other hand, had to beg her landlord not to evict her and her employer not to let her go. She's on thin ice with both of them now. She has been working overtime to pay off the medical bills for months. She never stops thinking about the ongoing impact her injury has had on her life.

I present all of that because this book will, at points, wade into the waters of discussing racism. In discussing racism, I do NOT mean individual experiences of race-based prejudice and discrimination. I will solely be referring to, and making analogies about, systemic oppression. While everyone faces some form of discrimination in their lives, oppression is a matter of subjugation and/or persecution by a privileged class.

Both in this book, and in my life, I will neither make nor accept the false equivalency of race-based prejudice and racism. Please understand, I don't condone either one, but they are not the same.

Both hurt...but one has a casual and longstanding ability to impact your employment, your housing, your livelihood, your health, and your safety.

Both feel unwelcoming...but one is created and enforced by politicians, law enforcement officers, real estate agents, employers, bankers, lawyers, and doctors. People of privilege and authority have created a culture that enforces permanent race-based, second-class citizenry. These are not just individual people being jerks to one another for arbitrary reasons.

THE FORMAT OF THIS BOOK...

This book is about the intersection of race and polyamory.

Just so you understand: This isn't a beginner's guide to polyamory. It's more of a beginner's guide to what polyamory looks like for underrepresented polyamorists.

It's a book about changing the contrast of your social circle and your local polyamory community, and why this is an important thing to do. It's basically a sociology book that uses polyamory as its focus.

I enjoy lots of things about polyamory, but some of my favorite things include the lessons I learn in navigating multiple relationships and transfer to every other aspect of my life. These aspects include all of the communication skills, the emotional literacy, the creation of boundaries, the scheduling, and the confronting of harsh realities. All of these aspects are practiced on a regular basis among people I love. All of these aspects are tested in the world outside of my relationships.

The same can be true of this book.

While this book is about how race plays out in polyamorous communities, much of it will translate to situations and groupings and lifestyles far outside of ethical non-monogamy. That's a good thing. One more tool in the toolbelt…regardless of the project at hand.

Now, when I speak about the topic of racial diversity at conferences, it's less of a lecture and more of a led discussion. There's a reason for this. I've been dealing with the societal construct of race my whole life. It's defined how I see the world and informed how the world sees me. It can't be ignored. It's always a factor for me. As such, I have a ton of stories, from my childhood to today, that play out how my race has factored in on some daily operation. But since I'm not the only one with these experiences, my speaking engagements are also about inviting others to tell their stories as well.

Just as I do in these workshops, I will cover a lot of topics in this book.

I will address specific barriers for entry — unarticulated disadvantages and unintentional difficulties — that people of color face in polyamory communities and alternative-lifestyle communities, in general.

I will discuss the source of people's discomfort in talking about race.

I will lay out ideas for how we can foster and appreciate diversity in our communities.

The magic of these conversations, when had in person, is that as I explain a specific point, I can usually add a personal story of how I was affected by that point in real life…and then someone else does, too. The topic becomes "real" as real people speak their truths. The topic also becomes "real" as real people see themselves on the wrong side of the story.

For instance, if I discuss how I was fetishized at an event, not only will more people chime in about how they were also fetishized at separate events, other attendees will realize that fetishization was something they've unknowingly contributed to. It can be a bit of a rude awakening to hear your own behavior used as a model for bad behavior.

One of the main problems, at the intersection of race and polyamory (and really at the intersection of privilege and oppression), is that we don't always know what we're doing, we don't always stop talking long enough to listen, and we're often far too scared or too defensive to learn uncomfortable truths about ourselves or our behaviors. This is the reason why a few of my workshops have led to tears and uneasy feelings. That's not a bad thing though. We all have room to grow, and you don't get to enact social change while sitting in a comfortable spot.

To mimic the discussion-based tone of my in-person workshops, this book will include accounts of people's personal experiences with the topics I cover in each chapter. Some of these stories will be my own. Some of these stories will be written anonymously.

All of these stories will be true.

I'm hoping that you'll do the next bit on your own. If you see yourself in any of these stories or find that you've got experience with any of these topics...***please talk about it.*** Don't let discomfort silence you when your voice can lead to a better situation for all of us. Trouble breeds under cover of darkness and, to paraphrase Louis Brandeis, sunshine is the best disinfectant.

Polyamory offers a wealth of unique perspectives. My partners have changed my life in more ways than I can count, but so have the communities that I've included myself in. The meetup groups I've attended, the polyamory-based happy hours, the online forums, the comments section to that one article that got shared on Facebook that time.

Use all of these resources to further the discussion...even if it makes you uneasy to do so.

Especially if it makes you uneasy to do so.

Talk to your partners. Talk to your community leaders and event coordinators. Tell your story on social media and invite others to make it a dialogue. Use every bit of access you have to speak your truth, hear the truth of others, and grow as a person, as a community, and as a culture.

Enjoy the book.

Alternative
Lifestyles
Be Like...

FORCED AMBASSADORSHIP

"A long time ago in a galaxy far, far away, I used to work at a 24-hour copy shop. I was the overnight guy working a 10-hour shift from 9:00 at night to 7:00 in the morning. Working that late, most of my responsibilities were about completing copy jobs that the morning and evening crews brought in. There's not a lot of foot-traffic in a store at 3:00 a.m., so, I worked by myself most nights.

The few customers that you do get, at that time of night, are usually people with special requirements: A need to create something in relative peace and quiet. A surprise project or a time-crunch that has to be managed in the immediate. Or, in the case of this telling, a desire for a personal touch or some conversation while working.

In this case, a schoolteacher decided to chat me up while she prepared the handouts for her next art class. No big deal, I like being friendly with the customers, and she wasn't really asking me for any help with anything. So, I continued to work on other people's projects as she worked on her own, all while keeping up a pretty steady dialogue. As she finished up and came to the counter to pay, she decided to turn friendly into familiar…and ultimately uncomfortable. 'Hey…ummm…do you have any pot you could sell me?' My face dropped. To be clear, I don't have any problem with the sale or consumption of cannabis. I have a problem with the assumption that I might be a criminal, dealing drugs…at my legal job.

I've got a policy in regards to racist microaggressions: When encountered, I try to calmly make the aggressor as uncomfortable as they've made me. So, I looked her directly in the eye and clearly stated, 'No ma'am. I am NOT a drug dealer. I don't have any drugs for you to purchase.' Then her face dropped. She had the nerve to be offended.

'Don't get that attitude with me. It's not like I'm a racist or anything. When I lived in New York, the late-night, copy shop, black guy was just who you bought weed from.'

We completed her transaction without another word and she left the store.

Compare this to a situation where a much older gentleman engaged me in conversation while he made his copies. 'Y'know, when I served during the war, we had a black fella in our company. Johnson! Now, I don't care what anybody says about the blacks, but Johnson was as hardworking and loyal of a soldier as anybody in that company.'

While perfectly pleasant, I had to wonder how this interaction would've went had Johnson been a terrible person or a lazy soldier.

What should've been a random retail-and-service job in my 20s, ended up being an enforcement of how the world views race and my place as a "forced ambassador."

All that these two customers knew about me was my identity as a black guy. Had I been a man of Asian descent, that schoolteacher wouldn't have considered me as a reasonable option for illegal activity. Had I been East Indian, Johnson's old squad mate wouldn't have given me the benefit of the doubt so easily…or maybe he'd have just used a different racial proxy by which to prejudge our interaction. Had I been white, in either case, I believe both customers would've offered me the advantage of individuality. Instead of referencing me in comparison to their friends or family or the countless other white people they've met, I'd have just been me… judged solely by my own strengths and weaknesses.

The harshest part, though, is that I'd have been surprised by it all if similar situations hadn't colored my entire childhood, adolescence, and young adulthood. For every one of these occurrences of forced ambassadorship that I remember, there's probably a dozen that I've forgotten."

- Kevin Patterson, Retired Renegade
Counter Jockey

The thing about finding yourself in a lifestyle community, like that of polyamory, is that there's a really blissful moment when you realize that you're finally surrounded by like-minded people. For the first time, you can communicate with people who share an experience…or a drive…or who just understand the language you're using without an explanation. It's wonderful for all of us who have ever felt isolated because of proximity to other polyamorous folks, or a prevailing religious ideology, or just the stifling social values of the local culture. You can just be yourself without being defined by that one element that sets you all apart.

This shifts a bit when you leave that community and go back to your standard environment, full of monogamous people. Especially if you're open and out about your polyamory. You may be the only polyamorous person in your social circle, or in your family, or at your job. If that's the case, the people who regularly occupy your space and time may look to you as an "ambassador…," a representative of all that is polyamory.

Now, given how broadly polyamory can be structured, and how diverse the inhabitants of these structures can be, it's completely unreasonable to expect one person or one relationship to be an accurate representation of the whole.

But here we are…and people of color are typically pretty used to the concept of having been the only person of their race in a particular setting. So, welcome to this new role that you didn't ask for, don't want, and can't really throw off without looking like an asshole.

The structure of your relationships, the success or failure of your relationships, and even your demeanor within those relationships will be used as an example by monogamous people talking about polyamory amongst themselves…forever. Or at least until those monogamous people see more varied diversity in the way polyamory is represented. One or the other. Even as a grizzled old veteran of ethical non-monogamy, I've gotten "corrected" about my approach to polyamory by monogamous people who knew someone who practiced it differently than I do. All you can do, if you have the energy and emotional bandwidth to do so, is be another example for them to work from.

So, when your cousin decides that they want to open up their relationship…expect a phone call about it.

When your married coworker needs help processing their more-than-friendly feelings toward the new office administrator…expect someone new to join you at lunch.

When your online video-game buddy just can't understand why their spouse is cheating…expect an advice-seeking Q&A session to occur the next time you play *Call Of Duty* together.

But wait a minute…polyamory and cheating aren't the same thing! Of course, they aren't. One is dishonest and shitty. The other is ethical and consensual. It's not exactly rocket science. But when you're a forced ambassador, you have to field people's backhanded compliments or negative, uninformed misconceptions…kinda like our favorite late-night, copy-shop black guy from the earlier story, right?

Another less-than-fun aspect of forced ambassadorship in the polyamorous community, is that all of your strengths and weakness will be tied to polyamory, and polyamory will be tied to all of your strengths and weaknesses:

"You look great today! Your partners must've picked out your clothes for you."

"You've been really tired, lately. I'd be tired, too, if I was having all that sex."

"I guess it's easy to manage all those relationships since you only have to be a fraction of a partner to any of them."

"I'm sorry to hear about your breakup. But I guess it was inevitable messing around with that polyamory stuff and all."

It's almost as if you're not a human being with individual attributes. You're just a conduit for polyamory. Fun, right? But that's why you're able to find refuge in that lifestyle community, surrounded by like-minded people. People who won't stigmatize, fetishize, or weaponize the one thing you've got different than them.

Except that, with that one factor out of the way, you may realize that polyamory is the only thing you and your group have in common. Just like any other group, you may find yourself separated and marginalized again...just by a different separating factor this time...perhaps race.

"There was an experience we had at a play space, almost two years ago. I was one of very few people of color in the space. We were doing rope play and I was rigging Ms. Pomegranate for suspension. So, I put up my upline [main support line], I grabbed onto it, and I swung back and forth.

What I usually do, is put up my support line, put up my ring, then do a pull-up and swing with it. That's kind of like my test. I walk around usually weighing between 255 and 265 lbs. In my mind, if it can withstand me holding onto it and moving back-and-forth, it will probably be safe to rig a suspension on it. If there's an issue with the rope or the hard point, I'd rather fall myself instead of putting a partner or any other rope bottom in a situation that could have a critical failure.

Well anyway, a few minutes after swinging back-and-forth on the support line, a dungeon monitor came up to me. At this point, I was already in the middle of rigging Ms. Pomegranate in a suspension. So, we were connecting in that scene and I was trying to put rope on her safely. But this dungeon monitor, an older black man, walks into the middle of our scene and says to me 'OK. You need to cut that foolishness out with you swinging and acting like a monkey. People are complaining about it.'

My partner is almost nude, I'm on my knees tying a hip harness on her, and now I've got to keep myself calm to keep angry energy from coming into and affecting the quality of the scene. But, at the same time, I've still got to deflect this bullshit that he's saying to me. I talked to the dungeon monitor afterwards and he said 'Well, there were people complaining because of your swinging. And I just don't want you to act that way because you know that they watch us when we're here. I want you to act the right way.'

At that time, I got really heated about it. But I cooled down and I thought about it for a couple of days. The thing that stuck in my mind, more than anything, was that he wouldn't have said that to a white person. He wouldn't have made the assumption that because I was swinging that I was acting silly or trying to get attention. He would not have passed a judgment like that on a white person and if there were white people that complained about it to him, then that's saying a lot about how I was perceived being in that play space."

- Kink and Sex Educator Mr. BLK of *The Black Pomegranate* at theblackpomegranate.com

A tough part of forced ambassadorship is when it doubles down. Part of the reason you might seek out alternative lifestyle communities is to feel comfortable around those of shared understanding; to get away from being different in a non-consensual way. But if you're immediately made to be an ambassador again, in regards to something like race, it can be frustrating.

Mind you, identities such as polyamorous and person-of-color are important, but it should be a choice whether to engage about those subjects. It should not be something that's a burden someone places on you. Especially, if "engaging" means being saddled with bullshit racial stereotypes that are expected to be responded to. And these responses are expected right in the place where you went to avoid the bullshit polyamory stereotypes you got while out in the mononormative world.

Forced ambassadorship also leads to "othering," which leads to a few different barriers for entry that keep people of color feeling unsteady in mostly white polyamory-centered spaces.

I'm going to get pretty deep into these barriers for entry in this book, so please be mindful. It gets bothersome to have to field your cousin's every inquiry about polyamory; it also gets bothersome to field every inquiry about one's race. Please try not to become a similar burden on someone else.

PRESENTATION AND THE ANGRY BLACK

"I don't even have one, specific, standout story about being the 'Angry Black Woman' because it happens so often. It happens the moment that I get passionate about anything. I get a lot of sighs and eye-rolls or the tone-policing starts.

'There she goes again.'

'Why are you so angry?'

'Well, if you just calm down, I could listen to you better.'

It's infuriating. Because I'm passionate or displaying anger, because of frustration with a situation that is constantly happening in different forms. So now, even when it happens on a scale that people may see as minor, it doesn't affect me in a minor way. So, I'm going to call it out. I'm gonna put it on blast. I'm going ask point blank, 'Will there be any black people there?'

To have people respond with a groan or an eye-roll... all I can say is 'Don't you understand how big of a problem this is, if I'm bringing it up? I'm not bringing it up because it

feels good or because I want to be an asshole. I'm bringing
it up because we need to talk about it and address it.'

Meanwhile, it would be completely different if I felt like
I was being heard. There was a time when I mentioned
the lack of people of color at an event. I didn't want to be
the representation or the person they all looked to for
black-girl answers or the face all over the brochure for
next year's event. I just wanted to attend and learn and get
what I paid for. Just like everybody else. Not only did the
organizer hear me and understand the problem, they took
steps to address it. The next year, there was a much better
turnout of people of color both as attendees and speakers."

– Dirty Lola of *Sex Ed. A Go-Go* at sexedagogo.com

In 2016, a black character was murdered in a popular television
show. I'm not naming it because **spoilers.** But, if you've
seen the show, you'll likely recognize the scenario.

This murder was the result of negligence on the part of
the corporation that was entrusted to care for this character's
well-being. In order to protect themselves, their public image,
and their financial holdings, the people at the head of this corporation took steps to delay a police-led murder investigation
until it could control the narrative. By this I mean hired image
consultants would craft a story that absolved this corporation
of all responsibility for the life they recklessly allowed to slip
away. They would withhold media access until they were able
to provide news outlets with exactly the story that they created,
presented by a source that they could make appear credible.

A part of the initial narrative control effort was to paint the
victim as violent and unstable: Someone who was worthy of
an unceremonious death. Someone television viewers and the
court of public opinion wouldn't mind dismissing. To achieve
this, the image consultants searched through the victim's personal history and social media presence looking for anything

they could use to further their narrative that this person was an undesirable. Was the victim ugly? Did they grow up with both parents? Were those parents citizens in poor standing? Was the victim raised in a "bad" neighborhood? Do they have a history of violent crime? Do they have any social ties to violent people? Are there any photos of the victim looking angry or wearing urban clothing that can be passed off as gang-related?

On the show, the image consultants were unable to paint a believably negative picture of the murdered character. The victim was too attractive, too worldly and educated, too well-traveled, and from too respectable a family. With the deck stacked against them in these regards, these spin doctors switched directions and instead focused on using the murderer himself as a scapegoat.

Using the exact same tactics, the corporation turned against their own employee and labeled *him* as violent and unstable. They painted him as a loose cannon who slipped under human resources' radar and abused *his* authority, leading to the death of someone under *his* care. He was then someone not at all representative of the ideals and goals of the shocked-and-blameless company that employed him.

It's all very sad…and then the credits roll.

While this is all part of some television show, featuring fictional characters in make-believe settings, it definitely draws from real experiences to tell its stories.

As I'm writing this, there have been two highly publicized killings of people of color by police officers in the last 48 hours. And four more, over the course of this weekend, that have gone woefully underreported. Sadly, that probably doesn't narrow down the window of when I wrote this by much.

We see it all the time when people of color are murdered by the police — or by people passing themselves off as the police in that moment.

Before any available video is shown to the public — before we can see what happened and make our own judgment on what is and what isn't — the people with the power to control the narrative do exactly that.

Those with government authority, or finances, or legal representation, or access to media outlets, or all of the above tell the story they want to tell. Before we get to see video of an unarmed teenager being shot in the back by an officer who didn't bother trying to de-escalate the situation, we *will* get to see photos of that teenager making a mean face or a mug-shot, if available. We *will* get to hear about any trouble they, or their friends, or their family had in school. Then, we *will* get to see smiling photos of that officer in his or her crisp, clean dress uniform in front of an American flag. We'll hear about their spouse and children and any commendations they've received in the line of duty. Whether reality or fiction, these are both very extreme examples of an everyday struggle. It's all about telling a story to people with the ability to effect and affect change.

In the case of the TV show and the murdered people of color, it's about convincing voters and consumers to continue to support systems that subjugate oppressed minorities. In the case of alternative-lifestyle communities, to a much less dire extent, it's about organizers convincing themselves that the voices of marginalized people don't need to be heard.

I bring up all of this because when you're playing the role of forced ambassador, perception is often as important as content. Presentation matters. Important topics really shouldn't have to be about narrative control, but a lot of the time, they just are. In controlling my own narrative, I have to remain aware of how I appear to the people around me. The way people view me can reduce my effectiveness as someone who wants to diversify white spaces.

There is a pre-established stereotype of the "Angry Black." They are emotional, irrational, unreasonable, and looking to blame the world for all of their troubles. Beyond being negative and insulting, the stereotype is extremely limiting. It takes an intelligent examination of social constructs and turns them into a mindless rant. It takes legitimate concerns about representation and makes them into a fringe element.

Upon application of this stereotype, "Wow! Kevin brought up a problem that we should really discuss and work at solving" becomes "There goes Kevin. Making a big deal out of nothing, again" fairly easily. It's complete tone-policing bullshit…but it exists, so it has to be understood and worked around…kinda like the problems themselves.

As a way to guide the manner in which I am viewed, I broadcast my other interests as much as I broadcast my fight for social justice. You will see me post as frequently about new video games, blockbuster movies, and the latest roster moves of my favorite sports teams, as you will about injustice or inequality. I make it well-known that I can and I will and I do leverage my privilege as a cisgender, heterosexual male for the benefit of transgender people, queer people, and women. The hope here is that in acknowledging my own privilege, and using it to stand for people who face struggles that aren't mine, I can inspire others to do the same.

In May 2015, comedian Louis C.K. made an appearance on *Saturday Night Live.* In my favorite sketch of that appearance, C.K. plays Abraham Lincoln in a send-up modeled after his own hit show *Louie.* In the show, C.K. includes vignettes of his stand-up performances between scenes of a fictionalized version of his everyday life. As a stand-up comedy version of Lincoln, he says, "The only thing I'm really tired of is arguing with slave owners about slavery, as if they're not just f***ing a**holes. That's really hard. You gotta act like it's a 50/50 issue."

It's frustrating that the message needs to be tempered in this way. It's frustrating that speaking about diverse representation in lifestyle communities doesn't always stand on its own. But often the people you're looking to address just aren't on the same page. In many cases, organizers will prioritize shielding their own feelings of discomfort at being addressed about a race-related issue over the resolving of that issue.

So, you end up having to present what seems obvious, in a way that seems like just a positive option. Inclusivity has to be seen as a *benefit* to the community. The lack of diversity has to be seen as a *detriment* to that community. The person bringing up inclusivity kinda has to address a problem without calling attention to the fact that it even *is* a problem…and has to address the people who have the ability to solve that problem… without calling attention to the fact that those people created the problem in the first place.

This means that in polyamorous circles I can't just be polyamorous. I can't just be a part of the group while passively hoping that the demographics will change themselves over time. I've got to be black and polyamorous. I've got to actively be an ambassador for both…polyamorous to have access to the room, and black to change the dynamic of that room. So, I must always be aware that I might be the only person — or one of very few people of color — at a polyamory-centered event. In that space of like-minded people, I might have to call out that lack of diversity…while still remaining a welcomed member of that space. Meaning that I have to rock the boat and still find a way to stay on board.

If it sounds exhausting, it's only because it *is* exhausting.

Hand-holding those who don't share your cultural background to address the needs of people who do, is a tough task. When you are part of a majority or a privileged class, it's hard to accept that your needs and your perspective are anything but universal. It's even harder to understand that addressing the needs of the few won't suddenly marginalize the many. Those "majority needs" and that "privileged perspective" will also be acknowledged and accommodated. That's fine.

They just can't be the only ones in the spotlight.

As a result of the frustration involved in the process, specialized groups will also spring up. While, or in lieu of, waiting for mainstream groups to address the needs of marginalized communities, other organizations can — and do — appear to exclusively focus on those left underrepresented.

INTENTIONAL COMMUNITIES

"I mean, given what runners wear and the athletic nature of the sport, a little bit of art appreciation kinda comes with the territory. I'm not out there ogling or staring at anybody. I'm mostly focused on my own pace and breathing and whatnot. Even still, it's hard not to notice all the mostly uncovered bodies working hard out on the course.

I started running seriously in 2007. I had just gotten laid off for the first time ever and I needed some new activity to keep myself feeling alive and motivated. I took up running, and that quickly turned into racing. I was only a few races into the sport, when I noticed how few black women were out there running with me.

I had an understanding of some of the cultural barriers in place that might keep black women off the courses… hair upkeep and whatnot. But, at the same time, I also had an understanding of some of the health issues that dispro-portionately affect black women. So stuff that increased physical activity might aid with some of these issues.

Little did I know, a group called Black Girls Run was getting started in Atlanta. Over the next few years of racing, I noticed a marked increase in the number of black women on the courses with me. I'd travel all over the country to run, and there were always these black-and-pink BGR shirts. At some races, you couldn't turn around without tripping over three women wearing their BGR shirts. They'd take over the whole race and stack the spectating crowds with their own cheering sections. It was incredible.

When my wife started running and became a member of the local BGR group, I got a chance to get a closer view of how the group works. Their membership is open to all women, but they center the experiences and concerns of black women as an underrepresented group in the runner community. It's a really impressive movement…and I got a chance to say so when I met the founders of the group at a race they co-sponsored."

– Kevin Patterson, Recreational Distance Runner

Black Girls Run is a successful intentional community. Let's talk about an unsuccessful one. Back in September of 2012, Towson University student Matthew Heimbach sought to start a White Student Union on the school's campus, and the idea was met with some blowback.

Heimbach was quoted as saying, "We essentially want to replicate what every student union does on campus." This sounds innocuous enough, until you examine what it is that student unions actually do.

In American universities, student unions are important arms of the student-led administration that allow underrepresented groups to have a voice in how the school is governed. They are a political voice for the voiceless, as it were. They also observe and address cultural commonalities among activities and traditions.

For instance, an LGBT student union may seek to adjust the school's policies on gender-specific facilities and non-coed dormitories, or they might throw a wild party during the weekend of the local Pride parade. Both topics are things that the general student body may overlook, but a focused group would key in on.

So, why was Heimbach's idea for a group frowned upon? First and foremost, it's because white students aren't an underrepresented group.

Not even by a little bit. Bear in mind that this situation might play out differently at a Historically Black College or University (HBCU). HBCUs like Howard University in Washington DC, and Morgan State in Baltimore, which neighbors Towson, commonly have a majority population of people of color. On the other hand, white people make up roughly 63% of Towson's student body and just shy of 80% of their faculty. With the remaining percentage of each of these groups split among several ethnicities, it's pretty clear that the vast majority of governing representation is held by white folks. White folks who will see their own needs and perspectives as universal, while running into few opinions to the contrary. So essentially, there already is a "white student union" on Towson's campus. It's called the Student Government Association-at-large.

The student government association does not discriminate against, or otherwise racially segregate, its membership. The same applies to the student unions, although they do specifically seek to increase the visibility and accountability for the segment of the population that they represent. So, the group Heimbach proposed was simply a way to add even more white voices to a mostly white establishment, and further marginalize the needs of those who struggle to be recognized at all…the school's students of color. If Heimbach's efforts were seen as racist, this is the reason why. Oh yeah, also probably because he was the president of a thinly-veiled white supremacist group earlier in his time at the school. But that's none of my business.

What *is* my business is the work of Ron Young, who says, "[In the San Francisco area], there were very few people in the polyamorous community. And then the ones that wanted to explore polyamory had to go into communities that they were never familiar with. I'd have to get on a bus, or a train, or a plane to try to go to some type of convention. We've been disenfranchised for so long, a lot of us don't have that much money or resources. So, a convention might not be something for us, as an option."

In 2013, Young, discouraged by some of his own experiences, spotted a need and founded an organization called Black & Poly (B&P). B&P works to highlight and address the needs of people of color who are often left out of the conversation when it comes to polyamory.

"Part of the work that we're doing…" says Young, "…is to bring polyamory into the neighborhoods. That's ultimately what we're trying to do."

A common criticism of groups like Black & Poly is the idea that they perpetuate their own problems. There's a recurring theme of "self-segregation is as bad as exclusion." This idea ignores the perspective of people of color in both directions. Self-segregation…isn't segregation at all. Whether we're talking about Black & Poly, Black Girls Run, or any university's Black Student Union, these groups do not keep non-blacks or non–people of color out of their membership.

It's not about separating.

It *is*, however, about centering.

Focusing on how black people view, practice, and participate in polyamory. Whereas mainstream groups are typically led and largely populated by white people — thus centering white experiences that may be mistakenly passed off as universal experiences. By even calling it "self-segregation," white critics are essentially saying that "they're doing to themselves what we've historically done to them," which brings us to "exclusion."

Exclusion is more a matter of denial of resources; keeping people away from the good stuff. Creating an intentional community is about sharing a mutually acknowledged cultural experience. Black & Poly doesn't keep non-black people from having a seat at the table of polyamory, it allows people to gather and appreciate polyamory from a specifically designated perspective. The idea that an intentional community is an example of exclusion ignores the fact that groups that are actually meant to be inclusive often unintentionally feel foreign and unwelcoming to people of color.

"A lot of times when you have these white spaces, black people feel like visitors," Young continues. "When [black people] see B&P or my name on an event, they know there will be at least 10 black people there. It encourages black people to come out. Even when we throw an event, it's fully inclusive and we'll still only make up a small percentage of the attendees, but [black people)] know they will have people there."

The idea that these groups are unnecessary or that they further divide a small community furthers the notion that white experiences are universal experiences. As I've stated earlier, on more occasions than I can count, I've found myself as the sole person of color at an event for polyamorous people. Although we all had polyamory in common, once the conversations moved to unrelated territory, I've found myself struggling to stay engaged with others…or others struggling to stay engaged with me. It's not an intentional or malicious disconnect, but it's something that should be acknowledged, discussed, and understood. If spending time in spaces that cater to our cultural similarities can help us find comfort when we're in the spaces that do not, both spaces have a valid purpose and right to exist.

If an intentional community like Black & Poly exists, why should we make sure that more mainstream communities are inclusive environments?

Why does it even matter?

WHY DOES IT MATTER?

"The hard thing about talking about racial diversity in polyamory circles is that, a lot of the time, white people don't get it. Even in the online forums. You got all these people who have a perspective that paints the landscape. But they don't realize that their perspective paints the landscape. So, when you say, 'Hey, let's repaint the picture a bit to recognize other races,' they don't know why race even matters. They don't understand that it's already racial. It's just that it's racial in a way that favors them and excludes others.

They don't realize it, so there's a lot of pushback.

Being polyamorous, people feel like that's enough of a struggle. Like the diversity is in our relationship style. So the diversity in the people who inhabit that relationship style is more of an afterthought…or not a thought at all. So, a lot of times people feel like it's a distraction to call out the lack of diversity in the way polyamorous people are represented.

I got into an argument with a guy online when he refused to accept that people of color could have different experiences than him in mostly-white polyamorous spaces. He didn't say it in those terms, but he just kept asking why it mattered.

'Why does it matter that people of color don't feel like they had a place there? If they feel this way, it must somehow be all their own fault.' He was so belligerent about the necessity of having comfortable spaces for a wide range of people.

Then, when it was mentioned that people of color often go to groups like Black & Poly to feel better represented, he was angry about that, too. He made hostile posts about how self-segregation fractures the community…as if his own attitude wasn't contributing to the feeling of distress to people of color. Then he mockingly proposed the founding of a White & Poly group. I told him that with over 30,000 members, most of whom were white and a staff of mostly white administrators, we were already in the White & Poly group.

He just didn't understand why any of it mattered. And
I just didn't understand why he was so antagonistic
towards a concept that supposedly didn't matter."

- Kevin Patterson, Online Forum Shitstarter

In November of 2015, Justin Trudeau was sworn in as the
newly elected Prime Minister of Canada. Upon introducing
his 30-person cabinet, Trudeau expressed the importance of
"[presenting] to Canada a cabinet that looks like Canada." By
this, he meant that the collection of politicians who he assem-
bled was more reflective of Canada's ethnic diversity than any
previous cabinet.

Throughout his campaign and current career as Prime
Minister, Trudeau has stressed the significance of varied representation among his country's citizens and leadership. He's
been quoted as saying things such as, "Diversity is the engine
of invention," "Diversity fosters new ideas," and "Canada's
strength and vibrancy have long been built on the cornerstone
of diversity."

The conversation doesn't consist only of ethnic or racial
diversity, either. Trudeau's cabinet also included more women
than ever before. Of the 30 people added to the cabinet, half
of them were women. It was a first for the country. When
questioned about why he made it a priority to have a gender-
balanced cabinet, Trudeau's famous response was, "Because
it's 2015."

So, why does it matter?

In polyamory, we have a unique perspective on the lives of
others due to intimate proximity. Romantic partners tend to
feed off one another. If Partner A starts up a new collection of
comic books, there is an effect on Partner B. Maybe Partner B
begins reading from that collection or starts up a brand new
collection of their own. Maybe they get a better understanding of comic books and decide that they just aren't into them.

Maybe it's half-and-half, where Partner B enjoys the narrative but not the medium, and instead takes up an interest in film adaptations of comic books. In any of these cases, through the closeness of intimacy, romantic partners gain a greater knowledge of whatever their partner is interested in, and what that thing means for them.

While similar things can be said of friendships, that proximal effect is typically not quite as close and thus less likely to take hold. Having multiple romantic partners can lead to such a wide range of new hobbies, motivations, inspirations, and revelations. Each relationship can, quite literally, become a new learning experience. Not to say that they all have to be… but it definitely doesn't hurt.

Going back to comic books: Let's say comics are the reason you met and engaged with all of your partners. Each of them will have an individualized perspective of the merits of each book, each character, and the medium itself. So, even if you only come by partnership due to a narrow selection process, you still have a chance to broaden your horizons within that limited spectrum.

To a foreign-born person, Captain America might be a social commentary on nationalism and patriotism. To a feminist, there might be an under-examined indictment on toxic masculinity found within those same pages. In regards to race, maybe that big stack of Captain America comic books reads completely differently to a person of color who has a different view of what America represents. For the person who hasn't thought about any of these ideas, each partner can open a doorway into some undiscovered territory.

The racial component is what I'm focused on here because of some of the language we use in setting limitations to our dating circles. Online dating forums are full of profiles that include some variation of the phrase, "I don't date people of a certain race. Just a preference." As innocuous as it sounds, there's a lot going on there, especially in situations where someone is open to multiple partners. To box out an entire race of people — people with different skin tones, backgrounds, accents, worldviews, and personal histories — for the one thing that makes them common, says much more about the excluding party than it says about the excluded.

In the same way that Black Student Unions differ from White Student Unions due to social context, single-race dating preferences don't function identically in both directions. Dating people of color, exclusively, can be about finding representation in a world that generally lacks it. Dating white people, exclusively, can be about blocking out all outside influences except for those that are already seen as universal. The idea that someone would actively seek to limit their perspective in such an extreme way speaks, not only to how they see the world, but to how they *want* to see the world. In one case, it is a rejection of new ideas. In the other, it is a rejection of the ubiquitous ideas that society is built upon.

So, why does it matter?

It matters because we can take this same line of thinking and extend it beyond our personal dating circles. As a community, we should seek to create an environment that is inclusive of varying perspectives. Flat out, it makes us stronger. Diversity of thoughts and experiences opens us up to new ideas or to approaching old ideas in new ways.

There is also a population benefit to keeping your mind focused towards creating an inclusive community. As Black & Poly expanded its membership, other mainstream polyamory groups got similar bumps in membership as B&P members started exploring other spaces meant for polyamorous people. The same can be said of any initiative to increase access and reduce barriers for entry for marginalized groups.

Along with a boost in population comes safety and normalization. By which I mean we're still a global community fighting a myriad of stigmas, and it's much easier to face them in a larger group. Coming together, inclusively, not only gives us a larger support group with which to solve our problems, but a wider set of ideas on how to do so.

Also, the more of us there are, communicating from the point-of-view of our unique experiences, the less likely we are to face off against people who are completely ignorant of our relationship styles. Less forced ambassadorship for all.

So, why does it matter?

Because if this were a topic other than race, we'd likely be on top of it already. Or, at least, we'd be more involved and vocally supportive. Any viewpoint about the possibility of an increase in sexual relationships in polyamory, that is expressed publically or online, is immediately met with an outcry for the recognition, visibility, and validation of asexuals, graysexuals, and demisexuals.

There is never any shortage of anger in polyamory circles for those highly discriminatory, anti-transgender bathroom laws. A polyamory group in Toronto withdrew their patronage of a local polyamory-friendly swinger club due to their inability to properly support their gender non-binary clientele. What I'm saying is, when it comes to allyship for social justice issues, our communities are not shy.

We broadcast for those who need a voice!

If you were anywhere near social media on June 26th, 2015, you'd have noticed an explosion of rainbows. That was the day the United States Supreme Court ruled to legalize same-sex marriage throughout the country. Along with the rest of North America, there was a massive response from the polyamorous community, as the polyamory community is no stranger to LGBT folks. So there was an immediate positive reaction to the Supreme Court ruling, and there wasn't a single online forum or social network that wasn't completely bombarded by rainbow-filtered profile pictures.

Before that ruling, though, polyamory activists, educators, blogs, and online forums were paying lots of attention to the growing situation. There was no shortage of discussion, informative articles, and op-ed pieces dedicated to the history of what was being called "the new civil rights movement."

Support amongst the polyamorous appeared to be universal, both for the benefit of same-sex couples but also for the hypothetical impact that might be seen by those seeking "plural marriage."

Critics of same-sex marriage often cite the slippery slope concept as the logic behind their opposing viewpoint. By definition, a slippery slope is a course of action that leads to a set of consequences that were unforeseen at the time of the initial occurrence. So, as theorized in often the most-offensive ways possible, allowing same-sex couples to marry might create an out-of-control breakdown of the very concept of marriage. But this didn't really happen. Although many did speculate that the exact wording of the Supreme Court ruling might have left the door open for polyamorous unions.

So, "yay" to the supporters of the "the new civil rights movement"?

But what about the "old civil rights movement"?

The one that never stopped being active?

The one that still fights racial inequality at every level of society?

When the discussion opens up about race, "the loud and proud" often become "the silent and uncomfortable."

That discomfort isn't always just a quiet removal of oneself from the conversation. Many who would stay silent in regards to race, will only speak up in order to silence others. Regardless of the topic, once a racial element is uncovered, what you'll often hear are people trying to make it a "down the road" issue or a "let's put a pin in that and come back to it later" concern.

Oftentimes, when racial inequalities are calmly discussed, they are met with circular logic and hand-wringing. When racial inequalities are angrily discussed, they are met with pleading for calmer tones. It's almost never the right time or place or method or message or messenger.

So really…the most comfortable course of action is to never discuss racial inequalities at all.

So, why does it matter?

Because it's 2018, and despite how uncomfortable it is to talk about the racial inequalities, nobody wants their group to be *that* group. No organizer wants to look around the room at one of their events and see zero people of color. Worse than that, no organizer wants to be called on it in a public space. Polyamory is small. With people dating and connecting with one another on social media and at events, it only gets smaller…tighter…more compact. And it only takes one conversation about how exclusionary a group is before it gets a reputation for being just that. No group wants to be known locally or widely as "the group that is thoughtlessly, carelessly, or intentionally unwelcoming to people of color."

Barriers For Entry

WHITE FEMINISM AND POLYAMORY

"Before I got into in polyamory, I didn't consider myself a feminist. I was one of those people who thought feminism had already done its job. The more I got into in polyamory, the more I started reading about social issues and different kinds of activism. The longer I read, the better I understood that the battle didn't end in the 70s. I learned about intersectionality and different types of systemic oppression. Racism. Classism. Ableism. So, my introduction to these concepts was really through polyamory.

This discussion keeps coming up of whether 'poly' is an appropriate abbreviation for polyamory. Some Polynesian folks have said that the abbreviation makes it more difficult for people of Polynesian descent to engage with their own online communities without running into interference from the ethical non-monogamy crowd. Their request that polyamorous people stop using 'poly' has been going around, on-and-off, for a couple of years.

It took me multiple times of hearing it before it clicked in my head. Even if we changed our blog titles and hashtags, continued use of 'poly' in personal interactions would contribute to erasure in online context. That's when I said, 'I'm using polyam from now on.' Other people can do their thing, but this is where I'm standing.

So, it came up again in a forum for organizers, educators, and community leaders. Some people who I really respect, and some people who I thought were more progressive than I am, wrote things that were really disheartening. The Polynesian people who cited this as an issue were labeled as 'trolls.' As if they didn't have a right to be upset about something that was harmful to them. The conversation turned from finding ways to address something potentially damaging, to finding ways to invalidate their pain.

I went online and found people who identified as Polynesian and presented their voices to the group. All those people that the group said didn't exist. I brought it up and it mostly fell on deaf ears. People were content to just talk over people of color; to erase their experiences. Usually white people will listen to white people. It shouldn't need to be white people who stick up for people of color, in these cases. People of color should be able to say things and be heard, period. But... they don't. And this time white people who viewed me as a white person weren't even listening to me. So, the conversation was just completely shut down and they weren't hearing anything they didn't want to hear."

- Writer Jess Mahler of *Polyamory on Purpose*

Back in July of 2015, MTV released the nominees for their up-coming *Video Music Awards* show. Rapper Nicki Minaj took to Twitter to remark about how her video for the song "Anaconda" had been snubbed for the night-ending *Video of the Year* award. To put it mildly, the video was a tribute to the bodies of women of color. "Anaconda," its video, and even its cover art were the basis for thousands of tributes, parodies, memes, and op-ed pieces. Even a musically out-of-touch guy like me had to watch the video several times, just to stay in tune with all of the resulting discussion. Not that I'm complaining. But the song was a part of the cultural *zeitgeist*. So, why was it ignored for MTV's top honor?

Minaj's Twitter commentary noted that other videos, those from artists of different genres and featuring "slim bodies," had received nominations ahead of her own.

Taylor Swift, whose video for "Bad Blood" *had* been nom-inated for video of the year, chimed in. With a video full of skinny actresses and supermodels, Swift felt like Minaj's criti-cisms were aimed at her. In response, she remarked that it was out of character for Minaj to "pit women against each other." There was a lot of back and forth, with several celebrities and thousands of fans adding their two cents. Eventually, the two music artists apologized, or whatever, and moved on with their wildly successful careers. The end.

Cool story, huh?

So, why are we talking about pop stars? For context, of course. One of the most important commentaries about this Twitter beef came from a fan who Minaj essentially co-signed by way of a retweet. This fan, named Berenice, tweeted at Swift saying, "Stop using 'support all girls' as an excuse to not be critical of racist media that benefits and glorifies you." The point being that while Taylor Swift made this about women-against-women, she ignored the angle that Nicki Minaj, a woman of color making music that traditionally caters to people of color, also has to struggle against media that marginalizes her race as well as her gender. Minaj's increased struggle gives Swift, and other white artists, an inherent and unearned advantage on a playing field that should be level. Welcome to the intersection of race, gender, and pop-superstardom!

Now let's get back to the point.

Modern polyamory was born out of cultural rebellion. While group dynamics with shared resources can be traced back to prehistoric times, and versions of consensual non-monogamy or ethical non-monogamy have been recorded in the 19th century, the earliest examples of what we've come to know and practice today were a direct result of the sexual revolution of the 1960s and 1970s. It was built off of the second-wave of feminist movements that brought about the birth-control pill, abortion rights, and the extension of voting rights to women of color. So the acceptance of gender roles was being challenged in an unheard-of way. Add to this a combination of counterculture, dismissal of societal standards, an increased recognition of gender and sexuality variations, and you have the modern polyamory.

The advent of the Internet and social media networks was a major boon to the practice of ethical non-monogamy. Most of us don't have parents or grandparents to model polyamory to us. We don't have several centuries' worth of fictional or non-fictional texts to study in regards to how we love. There aren't many movies, or TV shows, or love songs about consensual non-monogamy that we can convert into watercooler discussions with our coworkers. Being outside the margins, in this way, can be lonely and isolating.

The Internet provides access to a wealth of knowledge created by those who learned through firsthand observation. Social media allows us safer and relatively anonymous spaces to discuss our relationships, our local communities, and our lives. The results of these relatively new communication tools are entire landscapes that attempt to produce larger context to our personal experiences. What may seem like a worry unique to your situation can now be explored with the help of others who have floundered or triumphed through similar circumstances. A shared culture of camaraderie, perspective-driven dialogue, and best practices became the norm. This culture became reflective of its beginnings.

As the origins of modern polyamory are intertwined with feminist roots, our communities tend to avoid some of the common criticisms of polygamy, which is the practice of having multiple spouses. Polygamy is most often practiced from within a religious context, and usually takes its form as a male-dominated landscape. That landscape is of a man with many wives (or "polygyny"), none of whom are allowed outside relationships of their own, and who are rarely allowed to have romantic or sexual relationships with one another.

Despite the representational challenges addressed in this book, contemporary polyamory typically bristles at the perception of being a playground for male-harem fantasies. Online forums become charged when presented with men using polyamory as reasoning to treat women unethically. These forums become hostile feeding frenzies when encountering cisgender, heterosexual men enforcing one-penis policies in their relationships. Unapologetic accusations of misogyny, homophobia, and transphobia are almost always the result.

But fewer and further between are the unapologetic call-outs when it comes to the problematic behaviors that fall along racial lines. Especially when we stray further away from obvious examples of racism, and wade into the waters of race-based microaggressions. People, who would style themselves as allies, then become defensive as their own harmful conduct gets examined. Like Taylor Swift, we're quick to protect against one type of marginalization, but fall short of even recognizing another.

Failing to remain cognizant of the crisscrossing of several types of mistreatment that some people experience, can make them feel unseen or unsafe. In 1989, scholar and civil rights advocate Kimberlé Williams Crenshaw coined the term "intersectionality." Williams Crenshaw, a leading name in the study of Critical Race Theory, posited that different self-identities are subject to unique social influences, such as privilege, entitlement, and oppression The overlapping of multiple identities then becomes subject to overlapping versions of the resulting social influences. For example, if women are burdened by misogyny, people of color by racism, and queer people by homophobia, a black lesbian endures a combination of all three.

Intersectionality is not only the basis of this book, but also the lens through which we should view our experiences with polyamory. As a relationship structure that breaks with societal standards, polyamorists sometimes view it as revolutionary, in and of itself, which is true to a certain extent. But some polyamorous viewpoints come across as being "just counterculture enough" without the hassle of any additional activism. Our consensual non-monogamy doesn't exist in a vacuum, though. Our varying self-identities impact the way we practice our relationship styles. We shouldn't ignore how this plays out for those who face an enhanced burden.

The term "intersectional feminism" is used to denote a viewpoint of equality with respect to how different identities affect the construct of gender. Some takes on feminism actively seek to exclude the perspectives of trans women and sex workers. Others passively ignore the perspectives of people of color. This has been derisively labeled as "white feminism." The definition is not simply "feminism as practiced by white people," rather, white feminism is about neglecting all but the lived experiences of privileged majority representation… meaning straight, cisgender, and of course, white. We are all coauthors of this narrative in some way, and if polyamory is based around feminism, it needs to be intersectional. In the same way that we need to look out for women in ethical non-monogamy, we also need to look out for queer folks, trans people, people with disabilities, the young, the old, the poor, and people of color.

As far as the representation of people of color and polyamory, there just isn't a lot of data on the racial demographics of consensual non-monogamy from the 1960s to the turn of the century. Even still, there is very little to suggest that the inclusion of people of color was something that growing communities placed much stock in.

An indicator of such, are the books and resources that we all come to value when doing research into our respective polyamorous adventures. Any *Google* search or quick ask around an online forum will confirm who has the dominant perspective:

The Ethical Slut by Dossie Easton and Janet Hardy
More Than Two by Franklin Veaux and Eve Rickert
The Polyamorists Next Door by Dr. Elisabeth Sheff
Open by Dr. Jenny Block
Sex at Dawn by Christopher Ryan and Cacilda Jethá

Polyamory in the 21st Century by Deborah Anapol
*Eight Things I Wish I'd Known About Polyamory: Before I
   Tried It and Frakked It Up* by Cunning Minx
Opening Up by Tristan Taormino

The last of which was the book that began my own journey.

All of these iconic books of ethical non-monogamy have been written by extremely well-respected authors and educators…most of whom are white women.

That's not to say that any of these authors shouldn't have written any of these books, or that they don't deserve any of the credit that they get.

But where are the people of color?

If the topic is about love and acceptance, why is the scope of representation so limited?

Why are so few respected names using their influence to raise the voices of marginalized people?

And more importantly, why are we so hesitant to address this in the same loud-and-proud manner that we address one-penis policies?

"Over the last couple years of trying to be a white person in alliance with people of color, I've developed a couple principles of behavior in my head that help me stay on track. One of them is, 'it is more important to be in solidarity with people of color than get things absolutely correct.' As it turns out, there will always be some reason available for one to choose to not act on racial issues. And my white perspective will make those reasons look correct or attractive.

So, if I fail to put a premium on acting in solidarity, I will rarely or never act on addressing racism. And, in fact, I think this is probably true of most well-meaning white people around race, and why they often fail to act against racism. Which means that a person acting or failing to act on issues on race is often more of a personality characteristic than something dependent on the particular situation. People of color note this, and pay attention to when white folks act on an issue or dismiss it, because their behavior pretty accurately predicts how they'll deal with race issues in the future.

All of which is to say, when polyamorous people and organizations fail to speak or act on racial issues that come up, which is usually what happens, people of color note that fact and proceed to bail, often without stating that they are doing so. And then we [white folks] wonder why our communities are so homogeneous."

– Pepper Mint of OpenSF and *freaksexual.com*

A major epiphany in my own view of feminism and social justice came when a meme found its way across my social media feed. It was just a simple screen-capture of a tweet from Toronto-based activist Steph Guthrie. It read: "When you victim-blame, be aware that in all likelihood, at least one woman you know and love silently decides she cannot trust you." These words resonated with me highly, through the lens of race.

You see, a truism of relationships, human interactions, and of course polyamory, is that if you don't create an environment that's receptive to the truth, people will simply stop offering their truth. Often, when issues of intersectionality are brought up, they aren't treated as legitimate concerns. Or they're treated as trivial problems that can be kicked down the road and addressed at a later date. Or they *are* recognized as issues, but they just aren't approached with the fervor or willingness to understand as some other points of discussion.

When the matter of racial inclusivity or representation comes into question, the reactions of white organizers are immediately under scrutiny by the people of color looking on. Even if the particular case is a non-starter, if it is treated as inconsequential without examination, the impression is that all racial concerns will be treated the same way. Polyamory can be really tight-knit; people are always watching and talking. Self-identities are important. So, a matter of interest that gets dismissed can just as easily feel like a personal dismissal. That rejected truth, offered from the perspective of lived experience, will appear less and less. Eventually that truth, and the person expressing it, will be gone entirely.

For example, Jess Mahler mentioned the debate about the use of the term "poly" as an abbreviation for both polyamory and Polynesian. While it gained popular exposure through a blog post from Aida Manduley, this debate actually started on *Tumblr*. A *Tumblr* blogger of Polynesian descent, going by the name of ActuallyPoly, spoke on their difficulties in finding cultural resources and fellowship. They expressed frustration because a search for the tag "poly" would return a muddied stream of results.

There has been quite a bit of back-and-forth about the origins of the prefix "poly," and about whether Polynesians even refer to themselves as "poly." For someone who can regard this debate as just a thought experiment, it is easy to dismiss the small number of Polynesian people who feel harmed by the use of "poly" for polyamorous. For others, such as myself, it's easy to spell out the full word "polyamory."

In my writings, in my social media tags, and in my general online conversations, I no longer use the term poly. My blog and its features were titled before this conversation came to my attention. But while I can't rebrand those at this late date, I've done my best to make it clear, on all descriptions and subsequent branding, that the spaces where I do use "poly" are very clearly designated for the discussion of polyamory. Thus mitigating any potential confusion to those seeking culture and resources for Polynesian folks.

Finding a way to secure the use of "poly" for the polyamorous community wasn't important. What *was* important, was making sure that Polynesian people felt heard; their discomfort understood. For people of color, in general, this level of regard can be difficult to come by.

There are certain conditions and nuanced interactions that keep people of color from feeling like a part of our polyamorous communities. Of course, this isn't solely applicable to people of color. But these barriers for entry need to be understood and proactively tackled. It's not simply a matter of saying, "Everyone is welcome," and waiting for the magic to happen.

Feeling welcome in a space is more than just about not being barred at the door. Inclusive environments don't just come together on their own. Somebody has to do the work to make them happen. And it's not like a touchdown, where you can just get the ball in the end zone and then walk to the sidelines happy with the six points that you put on the scoreboard. Somebody has to do the work to maintain the diverse, respectful space that was created. It's an ongoing, working process.

If you aren't being actively inclusive, you *are* being passively exclusionary.

OTHERING

"…[M]y girlfriend at the time had a birthday coming up. She had had a lot of bad experiences with birthday parties, in the past, so she wanted this upcoming party to be epic. Her current set of partners was a group she was really confident in. So, it was a really big deal, for her, to have all of us in the same place in celebration of her…and I didn't mind being a part of that. But I was 'the black guy.' My girlfriend hosted this party at a big beautiful house, filled it with all of her friends, and roommates, and lots of romantic partners, both past and present…and I was *the* singular black guy.

I knew, going in, that I would be the low-man on the social ladder. Although our connection was very strong, I hadn't been with this woman for very long compared to the other partygoers. Unlike all but one other person, another partner of hers, I lived far away as well. I knew it was going to be a game of 'get in where you fit in.' No big deal. I can usually find my way in uncomfortable situations. What should've been awesome and helpful was that a few of my girlfriend's roommates and partners felt the need to engage me in conversation, or to invite me into the conversations they were already having with one another, to make me feel like less of an outsider. It should've been awesome…

The problem was that almost all of these conversations had to do with race. We were all polyamorous. We were all a bunch of geeks, or interested in tech-related topics. Most of us considered ourselves artists of a certain type. We all had lots of thoughts about the current political climate and issues of gender identity and human sexuality. We were all friends with the same person and, in the case of my girlfriend's partners, we were all dating and sexually engaged with the same person. But, instead of introducing me to a dialogue about any of those things, this revolving cast of white and white-passing people kept bringing up race…as if I was supposed to lead a class on it.

It was just like the party scene in that movie, *Get Out*. So much so, that watching the movie drew my mind right back to this party and it made me just as uncomfortable. The partygoers didn't even bring up race because it was relevant to make a point during a discussion about something else. They would derail pre-established discussions to throw a racial curveball in there. So, because I was in the room, it became necessary to talk about a black coworker… because it might impress me that they're willing to work with a person of color. It became necessary for a man to mention that his ex-girlfriend, in a tangent that was only vaguely related to the topic being discussed, was black… with a glance in my direction. All of sudden, white-passing women with white-sounding names, felt pressed to take ownership of their non-white ethnicity long enough to justify the racist stereotypes they had just brought up.

It was so far over-the-top. I didn't want to make my girlfriend's birthday party, which was generally pretty awesome, about my own discomfort…especially because she didn't see most of it happening. It was really hard not to, though. Thankfully, I was in attendance with another partner who was aware of it all as it occurred, and made it a point to be a sort of emotional anchor for me.

If I were to ask any of the participants in this series of microaggressions about that party and my role in it, I'm sure our perspectives would be quite different. They might see themselves as gracious hosts who reached out to a standoffish outsider to make him feel welcome. Or they see themselves as an inclusive bunch of good-hearted liberals willing to acknowledge and appreciate our dif-ferences. From my point of view, they were trying so hard to prove that my race wasn't an issue, that they proved exactly the opposite. It takes a lot to make me guarded and standoffish, and these folks got me there pretty quickly.

While I'm extremely proud of my race, it's still just a part of who I am. I'm a billion different things rolled up into one human being. At that party, the only thing that mattered was my skin color. I made a decision then to disconnect from them. If I was going to continue my relationship with my girlfriend, it would have to go forward with minimal contact with the rest of her social circle. It was one of the clearest and easiest relationship choices I ever had to make."

– Kevin Patterson, Standoffish Outsider

Have you ever watched a show or a movie and found yourself reacting physically to a character getting hurt? Jaime Lannister loses a hand in *Game of Thrones* and you flinch uncomfortably and grab your own wrist? James Bond takes a crotch shot in *Casino Royale* and you squirm in your seat a bit?

You see, the way the brain is wired means people generally have a natural, empathic response when viewing suffering in others. In other words, when we see people in pain, the pain-centers of our own brains automatically switch on in-kind.

In May of 2011, researchers from the University of Milano-Bicocca released a study entitled *Racism and the Empathy for Pain on Our Skin*. The discovery was that, when white observers witnessed people in pain, their reaction was dramatically different depending on the race of those observed. For instance, the psychological response was lessened when these viewers were shown images of Africans in painful situations. The conclusion of the study was that a "racial empathy gap" was present. In other words, white participants in the study believed blacks to feel less pain.

The idea that blacks feel less pain is actually fairly prevalent. It's prevalent enough that law enforcement officers have cited higher pain tolerances in black suspects as a reason for the use of excess force. It's prevalent enough that further studies from University of Virginia, Emory University, and several other sources, have turned up racial disparities in the way medical treatments are distributed. White patients were more likely to be given better care and/or painkillers, compared to black patients with identical ailments.

Black people, in these studies, were suspected of having stronger immune systems or thicker skin or blood that coagulates more quickly. The participants, in some cases, were actually medical students. Future healthcare professionals, who should know better, were taking these racial biases with them into their chosen profession. Somehow, someway, a notion rose that black people were fundamentally different in some pretty ridiculous ways. Enough so, that our pain and suffering were diminished on a human-level.

That's some pretty dark stuff there. Sorry about that.

Let me try to lighten things up a bit with a joke that I occasionally tell among friends whom I love and trust:

"What do black people do when they watch TV?"

(dramatic pause)

"The same thing everybody else does when they watch TV, you goddamned racist."

Every time I ask that question, and to be clear, watching TV can really be swapped out for any mundane activity, the room fills with blank stares or even misguided attempts to respond correctly. Once I follow up with the right answer, uncomfortable laughter ensues.

The idea that black people have some distinct and universally accepted way to watch TV is almost as silly as the idea that they feel physical pain in some unique way. Even still, people always pause to ponder the question as if it's somehow legitimate. Then a brave, or sometimes tactless, few will try to give an answer that is almost-surely steeped in one bullshit stereotype, or another. This speaks to the same type of racial biases on display in the aforementioned studies about pain tolerances.

All of this brings us to the concept of "othering." Othering is unique in that it's a sort of Gateway Microaggression. It is the basis for most of the other barriers for entry that this book covers. By definition, it means to view or treat a person or group of people as intrinsically different from and alien to oneself. Another product of forced ambassadorship, othering takes a fully formed human being and reduces them to one thing…one out-of-their-control thing.

In all of its varieties, othering tends to be insidious because the people who are doing it don't often realize the full scope of what they're doing. In cases of well-meaning othering, the person committing it might feel like they are trying to build a connection with someone different from themselves. They might see themselves as a trailblazer or an open-minded soul looking to step outside of their comfort zone. That part is fine. The problem is the method.

By seeking to engage with someone based solely around the one thing that makes them different from you, means you aren't being welcoming. You are, instead, holding them apart from you. Keeping them at a comfortable distance. Making the interaction a matter of Us and Them. You People.

This approach doesn't allow familiarity to naturally occur. All other things being equal, you are telling this person, "When I look at you, I only see you as this one thing."

"I was in Toronto attending a sex-education conference. I gained lots of great information and met some really awesome people. It was one of the best times I've had in Toronto. Given how many times I've been there and how much I love every visit, that's saying a lot. One of my most-memorable moments of this particular weekend was when I randomly met another Bioware fan.

You see, Bioware makes these top-quality, role-playing video games. They're really good about rich storytelling, well-developed characters, and inclusive representation. I can easily sink hundreds of hours into any of their games, but my favorites are the *Mass Effect* franchise. I own all the games, the books, the comics, I even have a tattoo of some of the game's imagery on my chest.

I was getting ready to look for food, after a polyamory-focused workshop, when another attendee recognized my *Mass Effect* hoodie as I walked past her. She indicated that she was also an enthusiastic devotee of the franchise, and she just sort of invited herself to lunch with me. No problem. I love sharing my interests with new friends. We ended up spending about two hours geeking out about *Mass Effect* and also *Dragon Age*, another Bioware franchise. Whereas *Mass Effect* is about science fiction and space exploration, *Dragon Age* is Tolkien-style fantasy with swords and magic and shit.

At one point during our geek session, my lunch partner mentioned being glad about the inclusion of the character Cremisius Aclassi, or Krem, for short. She explained that Krem, a trans man, resonated with her as a trans woman. Having positive, mostly well-delivered trans representation in a popular, game-of-the-year caliber series was really important to her. I agreed, and for another minute or so we discussed Krem before talking about other characters and other aspects of the games."

- Kevin Patterson, Shameless Bioware Fanboy

The critical part of this story is that the woman I was eating lunch with that day, brought up her identity as a trans woman on her own. While I knew she was a trans woman, it wasn't something that I, a cisgender man, needed to address. As a fact, it just wasn't pertinent to our discussion until she decided it was. We were just a couple of geeks talking about our favorite video games, until it became relevant to mention that she viewed a specific character in a personally material way. And when we were finished discussing that character, we were just a couple of geeks talking about our favorite video games again… continuing a conversation independent of our other identities. It's not that our respective identities weren't important. They definitely were to each of us. They just didn't have any bearing on what we were doing.

Understand, my new friend opted into a brief exchange about her status as a member of a marginalized community, and what that meant in regards to the topic at hand. Then she opted out of that portion of the discussion, and the discussion continued without a hiccup. Had there been a character that touched me in an individually specific way, say as a black man, I would've felt comfortable broaching the subject with this woman. Mostly because I felt that she would've similarly respected my desire to either opt in or opt out of that subject.

Othering limits your perspective of a person to just the one thing. Avoiding this means leaving room for people to be themselves, without being externally defined by the one element that sets them apart. This doesn't mean pretending that element doesn't exist. It means understanding that your point of view on that difference is not the one that matters.

I wouldn't have learned anything about trans women by forcing it to be a factor throughout our conversation. More than likely, I'd have just created a barrier between us by forcing our differences to the forefront. Instead of learning about what made her and I different, I learned what makes us the same, by letting her identity be her concern.

In a lot of polyamorous spaces, the fear becomes that poly-amory will be the only thing you have in common with other people in attendance. This should be part of the connection we build, and not another wedge between us. Coming from our often mononormative environments, being ethically non-monogamous can make us the other. For this reason, we should be able to use that common thread to learn more about our similarities.

Take, for example, our relationships vs. monogamous relationships. Typically, both dating structures include shared interests, communication, plans to go eat, and team decisions on what to watch on television. But that doesn't stop monog-amous people from bringing their clichéd impressions with them into interactions with non-monogamous people. We, and especially women, often face interest from normally monogamous people who understand polyamorous to mean casual, no-strings-attached sex with whoever.

Just like we have to defend against someone's determination to heap their misconceptions onto our relationship styles, people of color face that same struggle. We end up being othered in a group of others, all in the name of making us feel comfortable among a group of strangers. It takes awareness of the issue, and an introspective approach, to keep from being someone's cautionary tale about why they never came back to the monthly meetup.

DATING PREFERENCES

"As a kid, and in my teens, I watched a lot of TV shows and lots of movies. MTV was still popular for its music content. So, I watched lots of music videos, too. It wasn't hard to pick up on who was determined to be hot and who was determined to be not. At my age, growing up, we had Michelle Pfeiffer, Kim Basinger, Julia Roberts, Cindy Crawford, Nicole Kidman. Then the beautiful people lists would toss in Halle Berry just to say they've got some diversity.

I just sort of accepted the beauty standards that I was given to work with. Those beauty standards being young, thin, tall, and white with long, straight hair. Growing up in a mostly white suburb, with people who were also predominantly fed that same standard, I was never challenged on those attractions. There were enough people to fit the standard. So, why question it, right? I'm African-American, so sometimes I just substituted white with black. But the rest remained unchanged.

When it came time to go to college, I decided to go to a Historically Black College, partially to get a better understanding of myself. In an environment that didn't value as highly long, straight hair or slim physiques or whiteness, my own perception began to change. The things that I had previously defined as attractive were still attractive, but that list stopped being nearly as limited. I just got used to not looking for the same things in the people I wanted to be with. I'd start talking to someone and I'd find them attractive and then I'd have to remember that they didn't fit in that tiny box that society had drawn for me.

By the time I graduated from college, I was dating the woman I would go on to marry. She didn't and never would fit the beauty standards that I arrived at school with. But she's gorgeous and absolutely amazing and everyone I'm around can spot it. I feel pretty damn silly ever allowing myself to be confined to a standard that didn't accept this woman as beautiful. It wasn't just that the standards weren't mine…that they were given to me by society…it was that they were arbitrary as fuck. There was so much that I found value in, in a partner, that had nothing to do with physique, hair length, skin color, etc.

After my wife and I opened our relationship, I never stopped socializing and dating outside of my original notions of beauty. Almost none of my partners do, or have landed inside of traditional beauty standards. And that's not a bad thing. It means I'm not limiting my selection process based on something potentially meaningless."

- Anonymous

So, what do actors Idris Elba and Jesse L. Williams, musicians Jidenna and Lenny Kravitz, athletes Mario Balotelli and Steph Curry, and politicians Cory Booker and Lindsay Blackett all have in common with the author of this book?

We're all handsome black guys.

What don't we have in common?

Basically anything else.

These people that I selected, pretty much at random, all come from different family backgrounds. Different socioeconomic statuses. Different interests, occupations, and activist tendencies. We're from a few different countries and, despite our universal blackness, we've even got different skin tones.

I bring all of this up because I wanted to further examine racial exclusion in dating practices. I touched upon this concept a bit in the chapter about why inclusivity matters. While looking through online dating profiles, I've frequently run into phrases similar to this: "I only date white people. I'm not racist. It's just my preference." Every time I see some variation of that line, my first thought is of dozens of random attractive people with whom I only have blackness or maleness in common. If I'm viewing a dating profile filled with shared interests, hobbies, and values, but my race is seen as the solitary boundary to potential attraction, this sounds like more than just a preference. Something else is happening there.

I'm not the only one looking at this, of course. There is an endless wealth of evidence and resources on the topic; ranging from the scientific to the anecdotal. In an article for *The Establishment,* dating coach Emma Tessler stated, "When asked during in-person meetings, 90% of my clients report having racial preferences....of the 90% of the reported racial preferences, 89.9% are preferences for white people. And I'm not just talking about white-on-white preferences. I'm talking about all my clients, only 55% of whom identify as white.... when I say 'all my clients,' I do mean clients of all sexual orientations."

Christian Rudder, co-founder of popular dating site *OkCupid,* is widely known for using the site's metrics as a measure when discussing race as a factor for dating success. In the blogs and in the book based on that data, Rudder has reported that black users have a far harder time generating responses to their profiles or messages. Dating apps, such as *Tinder, Grindr,*

Plenty of Fish, and *Scruff,* have multiple blogs dedicated to screen-capturing and spotlighting profiles or interactions that include racist commentary.

In 1995, researchers wrote a study called *Ethnocentrism in Dating Preferences* wherein a sample of Asian-Americans, African-Americans, Latinx-Americans, and Euro-Americans was used to study attraction as a matter of societal conditioning. Several subsequent studies would boast similar findings. Our inclinations toward potential partners were found to be based more on the perceived approval of our family and peers than on similarity of values or physical attractiveness. Not to say that those other factors were deemed unimportant, but social status and perception of such were given higher priority.

Also given higher priority, were white people. They received more favorable ratings than the other three groups in the study, across the board. Asian and Latinx participants rated whites as more physically attractive than members of their own race. Blacks and Latinx participants viewed whites as of a higher status. These results do not exist in a vacuum. With the sample being exclusively American, is it any surprise?

Our media and popular culture are packed-to-bursting with negative stereotypes about people of color. Politicians openly and unapologetically slander Americans of Latin descent. Asian and East Indian performers rarely appear on American television or in Hollywood films. When they do, they are almost never seen as lead characters or in romantic relationships. Muslim and Middle-Eastern actors are either cast as terrorists or some otherwise offensive bundle of stereotypes. Black people in America have a long history of dehumanizing treatment and portrayal in the news, in fiction, and in society at large. Marginalization runs deeps in the representation of people of color.

Meanwhile, white Americans are constantly promoted as the standard of beauty and success and professionalism and variety. So, if one group is being rated highly, that means other groups...the ones consisting of people of color...are being rated poorly. If these easily recognizable patterns are based solely on perception of race, the only conclusion is that the disparity is based in racism.

Now, this isn't about type. Type usually reads as a composite of shared interests and compatible personality traits. For example, I tend to find myself attracted to the Venn-diagram sweet spot of goofy, geeky, gamer girls in glasses, and strong-willed intersectional feminists. While I don't limit myself to those types, those are the women with whom I've had some of my most fulfilling relationships. If I encounter someone, who I recognize as attractive and who fits that particular combination of characteristics, but I decline to pursue them based on their race, there are some follow-up questions that I need to ask myself.

Some may try to equate their preference for, or aversion to, a particular race to a predilection toward a specific eye or hair color. While there may be some predisposition to such things, it's clear that there isn't the same manner of stigma or favoritism wrapped around those aesthetic features. I imagine it's extremely rare to find anyone who would refuse to date someone, to whom they were otherwise attracted, due to their hazel eyes or dark hair. It's fairly common to find people who would practice that manner of exclusivity, in regards to race, though. And while hazel eyes all look like eyes that are hazel, blacks are a demonstrably varied peoples. The same level of variance being applicable to every race.

The use of this false equivalency is just a way to maintain a racially-informed worldview without acknowledging the source of that worldview. It is a way to walk away from the conversation without feeling like a bigot. I get it and I understand. No good-hearted, well-meaning human wants to believe that any part of their lives is shaped by oppressive instincts. As Tessler says, "This isn't personal. It's cultural, it's national, and it's fucking everywhere."

But calling someone a racist and saying that the way they see the world is informed by racism are two different things… and that is a conversation that shouldn't be avoided. The same can be said of the false equivalency of racial preference to sexual orientation. Your sexual orientation is not under your control. Now, just because you didn't specifically define the beauty standards to which you subscribe, doesn't mean that they can't be redefined. More on that in a minute.

"Ugh…this dude. I was at a TNG night. The Next Generation is for 18-35 year olds who are interested in kink. This was in downtown Baltimore. We were in the trendy part of the city, but it's still Baltimore. It's a 63% black city. Super black. The TNG night was about half-and-half, as far as diversity of white people and people of color attending.

So, I'm new to the event and this black dude comes in with a group of white people. They were all long-time attendees and it was clear that they were very into new people…like the guy wanted to talk to people who hadn't heard his spiel already. He was talking to me and I wasn't into it, because he was younger than the people I like to play with. Between his looks and his attitude, everything about him read as too young for me.

I don't remember how it came up, but as he was trying to hit on me, he says 'I don't really date black chicks because they're real messy and real high-maintenance. They have too much baggage.' I just stared at him blankly. What was I supposed to say to that? He was clearly trying to put black women down to score points with me, a white girl, and I was NOT interested. I don't know why he thought that approach was going to work. But he sure tried it. After that, I just sort of disengaged with him and stayed away from him.

It made me super uncomfortable. Suddenly, I'm in this place where I'm supposed to confirm or deny what he's telling me? I'm brand new to this space. I've never been here. And now, it's my job to tell this guy that he's a fuckboy or to walk away. He clearly thought that his misogynoir would put me at ease or something. Maybe he's been doing that for years. Maybe he's gotten a positive reaction from separating himself from blackness. But, it did not work at all for me.

There were a lot of gorgeous black women at that TNG night, too. He was missing out."

- Kay

As racism only works in one direction, racist dating preferences only work in one direction. That doesn't mean that exclusionary dating practices don't all require some manner of introspective examination. Whether they are feeding off of it, or practicing it, or avoiding it, all of these dating preferences are informed by racism.

In the story, a young black man expressed his preference for dating white women by appealing to racism. Using misogynoir, joint racial and gender bias targeted at black women, he hoped to receive validation from the woman he was pursuing.

Speaking about her own experiences with misogynoir, Cate Nelson says, "I don't have any specific preferences, but when I date black men, I make sure that they don't only date white women. My son's father did and I didn't realize it at the time. It was years later. I was looking back and remembered some of the things he said. It was one of the many things that drove us apart. I didn't want to shelter that hatred of self or that hatred of black women. And I don't want that to pass on to our son."

People of color sometimes actively avoid engaging in relationships with people of color of different races. The same standards apply to social-network approval, similarity, and familiarity having a higher bearing than physical attractiveness.

Cultural misconceptions have precedence over the reality of interpersonal connections.

Similar to the way intentional communities can be about centering the voices of underrepresented people, the same can be true in dating. As whites and people of color in America do not have symmetrical racial experiences, the same parallels can't be drawn from seemingly similar restrictions. They are informed by the same social construct of systemic oppression, but they are going in two clear directions. A person of color who chooses to only date other people of color or others of their own race, may be seeking to insulate their romantic relationships from the prevalence of a majority society they see as oppressive and problematic. Even still, that does not remove the need for an introspective approach. Refusal to accept inclusivity should never be a decision met casually.

Determination to promote inclusivity shouldn't be casual either. It should be actively embraced and sought after. So, how does that function in terms of dating? Well, one of the key components to attraction is "closeness." So, get close.

Studied as early as the 1870s, the mere-exposure effect is the occurrence of people becoming attracted to that which they've formed close associations with. Also known as the familiarity principle, the concept found its greatest and most-accepted amount of research through the work of Polish-born American social psychologist Robert Zajonc.

Zajonc's findings were that "mere repeated exposure of the individual to a stimulus is a sufficient condition for the enhancement of his attitude toward it." Meaning, the more time you spend with something, the more likely you are to regard that thing positively. In the instance of human interaction, the same holds true. Spending time around people who register as "other," rewrites your perception of those people. It replaces the stigmas and the stereotypes with actual lived experience. This is really important if you remember that these stigmas and stereotypes only exist to keep us separated as people. Their only purpose is to reduce us from being humans to being bundles of misconceptions; misinterpreted and ultimately mistrusted by those around us.

Another interesting idea promoted by Zajonc's work is that decision-making isn't powered by cognitive reasoning. Humans actually tend to observe a stimulus, have a gut reaction, and react. Only later do they try to rationalize that reaction. You see it all the time as people attempt to find logical reasons to justify their exclusionary dating preferences. The fact is, those snap judgments on who is or isn't reasonable for dating, are often based on the limited information of race and racial bias. So, if you seek to rewrite that script, you're simply going to need more information.

It's easy to practice polyamory while maintaining the same exclusionary bubble, but it doesn't have to be that way. Of course, I'd never suggest dating people as a social experiment. In fact...don't. Don't do that. What you can and should do is promote inclusive environments in your polyamory community. Go to events and conferences that center underrepresented voices. You should seek out diverse groupings in your hobbies and special interests. You should make friends. Find common ground with people who don't look like you or don't live like you. Normalize variety in your everyday life. The rest takes care of itself.

Polyamory has a built-in feature of bringing people together. Through interconnected romances, friendships, sexual dalliances, and any combinations therein, we have the ability to easily stretch outside of our comfort zones. People who might've existed forever outside of our social circles often end up as metamours or as friendly faces at our local meetups. Don't lose the opportunity to learn more about others and ultimately about yourself.

BREAKDOWNS IN REPRESENTATION AKA WHITE PEOPLE SHIT

"I grew up in a white neighborhood. I moved there when I was in 4th grade. So, I went from a relatively mixed community in Alabama to a majority-white suburb of Houston, Texas. So, I was oftentimes the only black person that a white person had met in real life. All of their interactions with black people were based on television and, at that time, portrayals of blacks weren't very positive. As far as popular media, there was *The Cosby Show* and that was pretty much it. It was pretty isolating.

So, growing up as a kid, you're looking to find people you identify with. For me, I didn't really see that. What I remember very clearly, was watching cartoons after school and on Saturday mornings. You'd see all of these superheroes and other characters and the vast majority of them were white. Mostly white males and occasionally white females.

I'd immediately gravitate towards the few black characters that you had. Doc and Roadblock from *G.I. Joe* or all of those black characters that Cree Summer voiced. It was to the point where I had to attribute blackness to characters that weren't explicitly so. Characters that weren't even human, but were a little off-color or a little darker or had a little bass in their voices became black. Good examples were Panthro from *ThunderCats*, Blaster, Jazz, and Optimus Prime from *The Transformers*, even Papa Smurf. These were characters that I could identify with. They were ambiguous enough that I claimed them. I wasn't given the representation, I just had to create it for myself.

Lack of representation was still a big issue for me, all the way through my teens and into adulthood. I went to high school with about 3,000 kids and roughly 50 of us were black. I had lots of friends, but the racial aspect still made it a lonely experience. The representation wasn't there in my real life or my fantasy life, and it was difficult to find a place to fit into either.

It's why I gravitated towards the DC Comics imprint Milestone Media. It finally offered a diverse set of creators who put together a wealth of black, Spanish, and Asian superheroes. They even had a lot of LGBT characters about two decades before it became popular to do that. It's also why I ended up attending an HBCU when it came time to select a college. I just wanted to see myself reflected in my environment...both real and fictional."

- "Cpt. Gerald Lipsomb" of the U.S. Air Force

I'm going to perform a quick and informal experiment right here on the PC where I'm typing all of this. I'm sure your mileage may vary if you decide to perform this same experiment, but I'm going to give you my honest results as they currently occur. The experiment is simple: I'm going to open *Google* on my web browser. I'm going to type in a search for the word "polyamory." Then I'm going to click the "Images" tab.

Here's what I see: First and foremost, the universally accepted symbol of polyamory, a heart with an infinity symbol. Meant to represent endless love, the infinity heart shows up almost anywhere that ethical non-monogamy is discussed. It's lovely on mugs, jewelry, t-shirts, even tattoos. Even I have an infinity heart tattoo, adapted from a stylized logo from the *Assassin's Creed* video game franchise.

On the same image search, there are several versions of the infinity heart. They are illustrated with a variety of colors and backgrounds. I see a couple black-and-white line drawings with appropriate wording woven into the design. I even see two versions of the symbol that are created using dragons wrapped around themselves or each other.

Other images available are graphic diagrams of polyamorous relationships. Most of these consist of colorful charts with brief descriptions of varying types of relationship structures. Above or below each description lies a unique ball-and-stick model that resembles a molecule chain. Thus the clever term "polycule" that some people use to label their dating networks.

I also spy various relationship configurations crafted out of those male/female bathroom sign figures, which are an assorted mix of three or more figures for each configuration. In some of these, a figure used might incorporate both the male and female form. Presumably, this is meant to represent trans or non-binary people...but it's just a stick figure, so it's kind of hard to tell.

Slightly easier to distinguish are the photographs of actual human beings who appear in my image search. The pictures of real people come from a myriad of different sources. Some of them are professionally taken family photos. Pictures that have been used in published Internet articles about polyamory. Others are promo-shots for movies or TV shows that center around ethically non-monogamous relationships. Several photos even originate from the websites of sex educators and group organizers who host, attend, or speak at polyamory events.

Looking through all that *Google* has to offer, I see several groups of three or more people in some manner of loving embrace: a three-person kiss; multiple four-person hugs; a big warm six-person cuddle puddle; two women making out while perched up on the shoulders of two men who are also making out.

My search definitely turned up lots of photos of people in bed. The people in the bedroom photos are typically naked from the waist up...with only a bedsheet to guard against the presumption that they are also naked from the waist down. The magical wizards at *Google* have also uncovered quite a bit of multiple-partner handholding, or multiple-partner hands on thighs, or multiple-partner hands making cute little hearts, or multiple-partner hands holding children.

There are a pretty significant amount of feet, as well. The feet are always bare, and almost always sticking out from beneath a white duvet. In July 2016, polyamorous philosophy professor Carrie Jenkins wrote a piece for *TheEstablishment.co* entitled "Dear Media: Polyamory Is Not All About Sex." In it, she describes the ubiquitousness of the boring and generic stock-photography trope of three pairs of bare feet sticking out from under a white duvet, and how often it's employed as a visual descriptor of polyamory.

There seems to be this prevailing thought, amongst the media and casual observers, that polyamory is just a "sex thing." Loving and romantic entanglements between complex and intriguing people are boiled down to the question of, "Who's doing who?"

Stock photos like the bare feet are meant to titillate. The articles that use them are often more about attracting readers than providing any accurate information about the real-life dynamics of a multiple-partner relationship. There's another element that was briefly touched upon by Jenkins in this piece. The element that I've really been driving at with this fun little experiment: The bare feet are always white.

In fact, the hands are almost always white, too. The faces and the naked-from-the-waist-up bodies are nearly universally white...or white-passing. Seriously, I hope your search differs from mine, because that would indicate a positive change. But, I was 56 images in before I spotted my first person of color.

Among pictures depicting real people and/or real human body parts, I was 16 images in before I spotted my first person of color. This doesn't sound so bad unless you remember that it's polyamory. So, most of the photos of actual people were comprised of three or more actual people. To put *that* information into context, I was 51 people in before I spotted my first person of color.

By the way, that first person of color in my image search wasn't even an ethically-non-monogamous person of color. It was comedian and author Steve Harvey in an image from his talk show, where he discussed polyamory with a man and two women who were all dating one another. In polyamory circles, it was the most stereotypical configuration available. A one-penis policy, closed triad, with one traditionally attractive, white, cisgender, heterosexual man, and two traditionally attractive, white, cisgender, bisexual women.

To dig a little deeper, and to go on a bit of a tangent about this particular image, the gentleman featured in that episode has repeatedly appeared in media that was supposedly polyamory-friendly. First, in online videos describing the structure of his triad relationship, then, in the aforementioned talk-show appearance, and most recently in videos announcing the simultaneous pregnancy of both female partners.

All of this content features this man's voice as the lead and his partners as background support. There's a reason for this. The man in this photo is well-known for his business and video series promoting dating tips and attraction techniques for men who seek women. Much of this gentleman's media involves artificially engineering social influence over women by leveraging their own insecurities against them. Steve Harvey, who has been accused of multiple infidelities across his three marriages, is also well-known for selling tons of books full of fairly misogynistic, extremely cis-and-heteronormative relationship advice.

So, in a *Google Image* search about polyamory, the first person of color who I encountered was a serial cheater, as he was giving an interview to a pick-up artist who uses polyamory and his partners as props, in a dream-scenario marketing tool for his methods of manipulating women.

This is not the representation that we need.

And representation is the point to all of this. The *Google* search, and everything it's uncovered, is all one big signpost that says, "This is what polyamory looks like"…or at least what mainstream media has declared it to look like. It's cute that we can talk about and dissect something as random and frivolous as a *Google* search here, but that's not where it ends.

"Well, in broad strokes, I saw this book about sex educators that came out, and I looked at the list of contributors and thought, 'Wow! That is one pale bunch of people.' As someone who is light-skinned Latinx, I know that just because someone is light-skinned, does not mean they are white/Anglo. But I happened to know a lot of the faces that I was seeing in the book. I knew that they were white folks. The ones that I didn't know personally, I looked up. So, there was no confusion.

I felt really discouraged that this was being touted as a book of 'masters,' and people with lots of expertise and knowledge, while including no people of color. Also, it was lacking in some other key departments of diversity. So, I poked a few of the contributors, that I considered to be friends, as well as the editor of the book. While I wasn't exactly friends with the editor, we knew each other as professional colleagues.

So, I reached out to a few of the authors, who I considered friends, to ask if they noticed that the book had no people of color in it. My approach, initially, was very personal and grounded in curiosity. But it was also grounded in confusion and hurt. A lot of the responses that I got were 'I didn't realize. I didn't know. I didn't take the time to gather more information about who else was contributing.'

While that makes sense on some level, given how busy we all are, it doesn't actually take long to check in about diversity on projects that you're contributing to.

In negotiating this kind of work, you have to care and put in the effort to change the status quo. I believe that personally and professionally. If you're committed to any kind of equity in this world, it is incumbent upon you and incumbent upon us to really interrogate the projects that we're part of. It is up to us to ask the hard questions that the creators of these projects may not have thought of.

It's something that I do now, for any project. If I'm invited to speak at a *Sex Week* or a conference, for example, I always ask the organizers about the other speakers they've invited, and the topics they intend on covering. I don't just ask either. I make it clear that I'm asking because I care very deeply about representation and equity.

There are events that need a bit of help in certain areas. So, if they do, I offer suggestions and recommend a few names. I make it a dialogue. It doesn't actually take much time, ultimately, but it does make a big difference in diversifying spaces that may not have otherwise been diverse, especially around axes that aren't as discussed, such as disability and class.

In discussing the book with its editor, the conversation started off nice enough, with a lot of me explaining the relationship race has to sexuality and why the book was problematic, providing a rationale for changing the book, and then jointly strategizing on how he might be able to do that ethically and with an eye toward justice.

However, interactions turned sour after the official statement from Women of Color Sexual Health Network (WOCSHN) came out, and his tone changed entirely. Though I had been transparent from the beginning about the fact we were writing a statement and what our framing would be, it still struck a nerve. Subsequently, the editor and his partner publicly called us bullies, shut down, and were very reactionary in their responses on their site, calling our tone 'offensive' and our statements 'inflammatory, counter-productive, deeply hurtful, and absurd.'

Those statements were soon thereafter revised, thankfully, but done in less than ideal ways (e.g. editing their original words and post without noting that any edits had been made, as if their kinder language had always been there – which is too close to gaslighting for my taste). And, while many people supported us, there was also a lot of private and public backlash, including someone spending the time and money to start a WOCSHN statement parody website, and another person writing a long-winded article that basically said, 'How dare you accuse a Jewish person of being a white supremacist?' As if that's what we said (we didn't), and as if Nazis invented white supremacy (they didn't).

On our end, this wasn't about shooting down the book, but instead calling attention to a problem endemic in this industry and in society, and asking our colleagues and our entire field to do better.

Thankfully, a revised edition of the book included people of color, but it was another example of people of color being an add-on and not an integral part of the process. It was another example of people of color putting in a lot of emotional labor and just general professional work into seeing a change. And to date, all evidence of their responses and this issue have been scrubbed from their site, which is very telling.

I'm glad the book changed, but in doing this work, it's not just about how the products look in the end, but also the process of getting there and how we are treated when we speak up. I believe people can change and evolve, that's why I bring these things up. If I had given up on my white colleagues, I wouldn't bring this to their attention. This is me saying, 'I know you can do better.'

This happens all the time, at pretty much every conference, unless it's run specifically by and for us as people of color. And some mainstream conferences are certainly changing a lot and getting deeply committed to anti-racism, particularly after this whole deal with the book—but there's still a lot of work to be done. I'm glad to see the discourse shifting, but a lot of it is overdue, and there's a lot of catching-up that needs to happen to reach any semblance of equity."

  – Sex Educator and Therapist Aida Manduley, LCSW

The fact is, when you don't see yourself represented in a particular thing, it becomes easy to assume that that thing is not meant for you. For people of color, these lapses in representation can start to fall into the category of "white people shit."

Growing up, I would rarely see imagery of people of color engaging in certain professions, activities, or habits. In some cases, if I knew a person of color who was involved in one of those interests, I'd be able to override the societal programming. In other cases, those pursuits would simply be written-off as "white people shit," and left alone.

These boundaries are seemingly arbitrary, and often self-inflicted within our own communities. Comedian Aisha Tyler, while being interviewed on the show *Totally Biased with W. Kamau Bell*, once recounted an instance of "white people shit" being enforced for a person of color. She said, "I was with a friend of mine. We were at a table, backstage of a TV show. He was eating a bagel and someone came up to him and said 'black people don't eat bagels.' I'm like, 'Bitch, are you telling me that black people don't eat bread with holes in it?'"

Something similar happened to me when a friend of mine, a person of color, was eager to explore polyamory. In a moment that created a forced ambassadorship for me, he suggested that his current romantic partner, also a person of color, spend a little time with me and my family. While attending a party at our home, his partner would be able to pick my brain on the subject, and see how we all function together.

I picked up my friend and his partner from the bus station, and the questions started during the drive back to the house. The very first one was, "No offense but...isn't polyamory 'white people shit?'"

They had gotten the perception of ethical non-monogamy, as something only white people do, from their media exposures to ethical non-monogamy. These exposures were to shows like *Big Love, Swingtown,* and *Sister Wives.*

While these shows feature other forms of ethical non-monogamy, from the outside looking in they might be indistinguishable from polyamory. If you've ever discussed polyamory with someone unfamiliar with the term, you might've already faced the mainstream's difficulties with interpretation.

What isn't difficult to interpret is that all of the shows I just mentioned are almost completely devoid of people of color in non-monogamous roles. The performers or featured personalities are almost all white or white-passing.

Also ubiquitous in these presentations is the idea that ethical non-monogamy is for the fairly affluent and the traditionally attractive. It all makes the perceptions very limiting. Now, when it comes to media that is actually meant to offer nuanced presentation of polyamory, the very same issues occur.

"Maybe a decade ago, I met someone who was in a polyamorous relationship, who was interested in dating me. I had never heard of polyamory. Ten or so years ago, it wasn't something in the lexicon. It wasn't in the open. Nobody was talking about it. So, this was the first time I'd heard about it.

I thought it would be an interesting idea to explore. I'm a writer and a filmmaker. So, as a writer, my brain immediately went off on several tangents, trying to think of ways of telling a new and different kind of love story. I'd never heard of a love where you were allowed and encouraged to love others romantically. So, that was what inspired the initial idea in my mind.

As a writer and a woman and a black woman, it is my desire to create dynamic, interesting, inclusive stories that feature black people and black women in ways that we don't get to see them, in narratives that we don't usually get to explore. I hadn't seen anything like that, in regards to polyamory or non-monogamy, that wasn't about a heterosexual couple being interested in another woman and forming triad.

I've only seen maybe one documentary where it was two bisexual men involved in a relationship with one woman, but that was a long time ago. In mainstream narratives, I hadn't seen anything like that. Even when I would see things about ethical non-monogamy, it was always two women and one man.

So, I wanted to play with that concept a bit. I wanted to show everyday people. Not rich folks or glamorous folks. Mind you, I think everybody in the show is attractive. They're good-looking people, but I really wanted to take the glitz and glamour out of polyamory and really deal with it as a family drama.

There are lots of families who come from different social-economic backgrounds that do not fit inside of certain relationship paradigms. I wanted to see what it might look like if you have a couple that have been married for quite a long time. They have children and an investment in monogamy, and have quite a few things at risk when making or trying to make a shift in their relationship style.

I wanted it to be real, uncomfortable at times. Not a fairy tale. I needed it to deal with the struggles that they might go through in making that sort of change – see the journey to the other side."

- Jackie Stone, Creator of the
digital series *Compersion*

Starting in 2012, the cable television network Showtime aired two seasons of a reality show called *Polyamory: Married and Dating*. The program's premise was a glimpse into the life of two separate polyamorous networks, consisting of three and four people respectively. In the second season, a new triad was added to replace the one featured in the first season.

The audience's viewpoint would shift, back-and-forth, between the two polycules, and we'd get to understand the unique dynamics of each. Both groups in both seasons were comprised almost entirely of cisgender, traditionally attractive, seemingly-affluent, white or white-passing cast members.

The show was hit with a pretty wide variety of criticisms. The titillating use of mildly pornographic sex scenes was off-putting to many polyamorous viewers. As polyamory often faces the stigma of simply being a type of sexual fetish, the inclusion of those sequences seemed geared toward the cliché and not the actuality. Much of the community's focus on communication, compromise, and autonomy gave way to various depictions of entitlement, manipulation, and partner-on-partner coercion.

Upon viewing the show, *Grantland*'s Emily Yoshida declared, "Polyamorist groups often refer to themselves as a family even if they don't have children. I suspect this is because an unusually high percentage of them behave like spoiled 8-year-olds."

Yoshida continued by calling out the show's tendency to cater to the heterosexual male gaze, "If you're a straight dude and interested in polyamory, but worried you'll be asked to have relations with another dude, don't worry — apparently only the girlfriend–wives are under any kind of obligation to swing both ways."

Truly, the show's strict reliance on the stereotypical partnerships of straight men and bisexual women appeared calculated to tap directly into common heteronormative ideas. These are the type of notions that devalue sexual relationships between women, and cast them as "under the ownership" of their male partners. Combine this with the program's complete lack of openly identified trans or non-binary cast members, and you have a show that's inclusive to only a fair few. It all gives the impression that the intended audience was heterosexual, cisgender, young, white men.

This narrow viewpoint of representation affects our ability to self-explore. A common theme that you'll hear when you listen to people's polyamorous origin stories, is that of the lonely closeted outsider. Often, you'll hear someone say something to the effect of, "I knew that the monogamous narratives I was being fed by popular culture didn't feel natural to me, but I didn't have a name for how different I felt, and I didn't have anyone to talk to about it."

This theme leads to tales of people feeling awkward or broken in their relationships. Periods of serial monogamy punctuated with the occasional infidelitous overlap.

So, what happens when these folks finally discover polyamory, and the visuals immediately exclude them?

What happens when the imagery makes them feel as if they don't belong?

What happens when the resources that they look to, in order to understand themselves and make sense of their uniqueness, leaves them feeling just as isolated as when they started?

There are tons of depictions of non-monogamy in pop culture that include people of color. The problem is that these depictions aren't typically of the ethical variety. Every few years, a new slang term takes form in regards to casual sex or unfaithful partners or finding someone new while already monogamously committed to another. In some communities, terms like "Jody" or "O.P.P." or "Jump Off" or "Side Piece" become exceedingly well-known. Meanwhile, terms like poly-amory do not.

What we're left with is a narrowing of perception, among people of color, that the only way to explore multiple relation-ships is to do so unethically…if at all.

In 2016, writer and filmmaker Jackie Stone created a series on *YouTube* called *Compersion*. The self-funded show is a family drama about a long-time married couple taking their first steps into the world of ethical non-monogamy. The show has a unique combination of features that set it apart.

First and foremost, *Compersion* centers the voices and perspectives of people of color. The main characters are also looking to date separately rather than seeking to form a closed triad. These features are also tied into a depiction of people just starting out.

Other representations of ethical non-monogamy focus on long-time practitioners. So, the mistakes being made by reality show casts are regarded, by the mainstream viewer, as common practices of seasoned polyamorous folks. In *Compersion*, the adversity is accepted as the early struggles of a changing paradigm.

So, if polyamory is meant to be available to everyone, it needs to appear to be available to everyone. The pushing of a singular perspective on ethical non-monogamy leaves people without a place to go when it comes to resources. This isn't necessarily the fault of the cast of shows like *Sister Wives* or *Polyamory: Married and Dating*. The producers of these kinds of shows bear some level of responsibility for putting sensa-tionalism ahead of realism for ratings. Although I'm sure that's the exact parameters of their job.

Just like the intentionality of a reality show designed as a ratings grab, if you want to create inclusive representation you have to make it part of your purpose. If you aren't being actively inclusive, you *are* being passively exclusive.

A decision has to be made to center the voices and perspectives of the underrepresented. If you *are* the underrepresented, a decision has to be made to make your voice heard, and to project your perspective out into the world. There's never a shortage of people who need to witness your experiences to make their world feel less lonely.

TOKENISM

"I was in Denver, a city I had never been in, to attend and present at a polyamory conference. The day before, I drove 90 minutes to spend the night with my girlfriend in her hometown. We typically spent every other weekend with one another, and this weekend would've been our time together. So, if I missed this brief opportunity to see her, it would be almost a month that passed between visits.

The morning of my flight, I woke up well before sunrise to make the 90-minute drive home. I got my kids ready for school, I got myself ready to travel, and my wife dropped me off at the airport. With all the moving around, I was exhausted by the time I reached the hotel where the conference was being held. So, when a friend suggested that I skip the opening festivities, I took his advice and slept through the night's events. The host's welcome. The keynote address. The party. All of it.

The next morning, a conference attendee asked me about a bit of flashy attire on the outfit that I wore to last night's party. The party that I had missed. I didn't know what he was talking about. I brushed it off and went about the business of finding breakfast.

As I was loading up my plate at the breakfast buffet, someone approached me from behind. This shorter person threw an arm around me and pulled me down into a kiss on the cheek. It was a lovely kiss. Turning around to see who was offering such a warm embrace…I saw a woman I didn't recognize. I'm bad with faces, but not that bad. This woman was a stranger to me and by the look on her face, I was a stranger to her. I had been confused for someone else. She embarrassedly apologized for the mistake, and a nearby friend pointed out to her, her intended target…another tall, black man.

As it turns out, me and this other gentleman are several years apart in age, and he looks almost nothing like me. But we were the only two black men in attendance for the majority of that conference. When I got a chance to speak to him later that day, he asked me about my polyamory-activism. As I described my work, he hit upon the realization that I was 'the guy with the blog' who other attendees kept confusing him for.

He was the guy with the flashy outfit that I was mistaken for on my way to breakfast. No one was expecting the strange occurrence of not one, but two, tall, black men and, apparently, it was difficult to tell us two mostly dissimilar men apart…even for those who knew (one of) us well enough to initiate unsolicited intimate contact."

- Kevin Patterson, Professional Body
Double for Tall Black Men

Go ahead and *Google* "college Photoshop black."

It's cool…I'll wait.

Ok, if you didn't bother *Googling*, or even if you did, here's what you might've found: In September of 2000, a story broke that officials at the University of Wisconsin-Madison digitally inserted the face of a black student into a photo of a crowd of white fans at a football game. This doctored photo would be used on the cover of their 2001–2002 undergraduate application book. In that year, roughly 100,000 of those books were released.

Another example that your *Google* search — or let's face it, MY *Google* search — might turn up is that of a young black woman awkwardly added to a photo of three white women on the website for the University of Texas, Arlington.

Aside from the very clear difference in lighting (the white women are outside in the sun, while the black woman appears to be indoors with artificial light), it's apparent that the original photo features three close friends. But their digitally-assisted, single-serving friend stands conspicuously apart from them. There's another social commentary here...but we'll get to that later.

You may also be led, via *Google*, to the Toronto *FUN Guide*. The *FUN Guide* is an initiative of the Toronto Department of Parks, Forestry & Recreation, to provide a resource documenting lots of fun, local activities for people of all ages.

In 2009, a decision was made to showcase the diversity of the city by way of Photoshop. The "father," in a stock photo of a family, had his head replaced with a poorly inserted head of a black man. Look it up, if you haven't already. It's pretty goofy.

There are lots of examples of this type of behavior, but let's bring it back to University of Wisconsin-Madison. All of these alterations were used to create a kind of pretend diversity.

The Photoshopped Wisconsin student, Diallo Shabazz, was a prominent activist for ACTUAL diversity on the school's campus. When he sued the university over the misuse of his image, he demanded that university budget funds be used toward the recruiting of students of color in lieu of a monetary settlement. Many of the new initiatives that this settlement created were vetoed or dissolved over the course of a few years.

So, the school officials seemed to understand the value of diversity. They understood it well enough to spot a problem with the way the school represented itself. But instead of making an effort to actually change the makeup of the school, they resorted to using "digital tokenism" to create the *illusion of diversity*. The officials chose the face of someone known for his dedication to and activism for inclusion, and used it to promote a false narrative.

"Tokenism" is the practice of making only a perfunctory or symbolic effort to do a particular thing, especially by recruiting a small number of people from underrepresented groups in order to give **the appearance of sexual or racial equality within a workforce.**

It's a cosmetic change in a place where a structural change would be more appropriate. It's both lazy and disingenuous, but so much easier than enacting real outreach.

Tokenism plays out in polyamorous communities in the same way it does anywhere else. A group built around the idea of connecting with like-minded people, is going to serve that function first and foremost. A polyamory-mixer is primarily going to be focused on being a mixer for polyamorous people.

Shocking, right?

But "starvation-economy" thinking often treats every attendee as a resource that the group can't afford to lose, as it attempts to become viable. Once that group becomes large enough to sustain a population, though, you have to be aware of what that population looks like and represents...beyond the initial reason for creating a group in the first place. So ask yourself a few questions:

Does your group consist almost entirely of women?

Are all of the latest event's attendees well-to-do?

Does this meetup resemble a gathering of the Ku Klux Klan (KKK)?

If the answer to any of these questions is "yes," it is not coincidental.

Something in the organizing of your event, or the group, or the community-at-large, is drawing a specific crowd. Intentionally or otherwise, there is something happening that's narrowing your demographics.

So, if the cultivating of an exclusionary crowd isn't a coincidence, the creation of an inclusive crowd can't be either.

And a nod to the few attendees from marginalized groups does not make more of these attendees magically appear. Using promotional photos that consistently show "the one black guy" in attendance is not the same as outreach to unrecognized groups. There has to be a point where the majority starts to care about, and address, needs outside of their own.

If your functions lack diversity, you've got to actively seek it out.

Tokenism is *not* the way to do this.

Instead of encouraging a conversation about diversity, tokenism closes that conversation. It actually works under the false idea that the conversation has already been had, and that a satisfactory resolution has already been reached. It is hard enough to get community leaders to take a look at the demographics of their local population. They often feel that if there is even a population to speak of, that's all that is to be expected of them. Their job is done.

An example of tokenism that I was faced with was my inclusion in an article for *The New York Times Magazine*. The article, titled "Is an Open Marriage a Happier Marriage?" primarily featured the stories of several couples who opened up their unsatisfying marriages. The bulk of the text was taken up by the experiences of people using additional romantic partners to strengthen and maintain their floundering monogamous relationships. To create this piece, the writer secured a wealth of input from a wide variety of sources. Healthcare professionals, polyamorous educators, authors of polyamory books, longtime practitioners of ethical non-monogamy and also, me.

My wife and I were interviewed, multiple times, about every aspect of our polyamory. But when the article was released, our contributions were almost nonexistent. What became apparent is that my wife and I did not fit in this story of unhappy couples. We didn't explore non-monogamy as a way to keep a sinking ship afloat. Unlike many of the featured couples, we didn't use infidelity as a gateway to polyamory. So, if the theme of the article was "Relationship Broken, Add More People" it might've made sense to simply remove us from the finished product.

What happened instead, was that my wife and I had our names and photos used, while our words were all but ignored. Readers of the article would gain almost zero insight as to how a happy, healthy, functional, polyamorous relationship might work. But they might assume that the black couple photographed was similarly as downcast as the article's other couples. Our only value in that article was to create a sort of fabricated diversity. A diversity in imagery…not a diversity in thought.

"When I challenged him about the event's lack of diversity, he got defensive. 'There were at least five people of color there,' he said. So, I asked him how many white people were in attendance. He didn't know. Of course, he didn't know. The party was packed with white people. Getting a headcount of them would've required more than just a cursory glance. He didn't understand that that was exactly my point."

– Anonymous

In Australia, feminist scholar Dale Spender researched whether men or women tended to speak more in mixed-gender settings. While her work in the 1970s and 80s is very binary-oriented, and might be more gender-inclusive if it were done today, the results were still very interesting.

Spender recorded men and women speaking in classroom settings. What she found was that men universally spoke more. Changes to the gender ratio and encouragement of the female participants did little to create a balance. Men always spoke more.

I mention this study because of the perception component involved in the research. When asked to appraise who did the most speaking amongst themselves, female students generally had a proper read of the situation. Meanwhile, male students believed the male/female breakdown to be equal when women had only taken up 15% of the conversation. When women spoke 30% of the time, the male students believed women had completely dominated the conversation. The perception, for male students, was that women occupied a lot more conversational space than they truly had. The expectation, for male students, was that women wouldn't occupy *any* conversational space.

The same is often true in regards to racial diversity in polyamorous spaces. If the organizers can spot a person of color — or several people of color — at their events, they often feel as if that diversity problem has been solved. It's someone else's problem; it's just one less thing to think about. The perception is that people of color are attending in larger numbers than we really are. But that's only because the expectation is that people of color wouldn't be there at all. This is why it's important to talk to organizers about exactly this issue. If it is their aim to cater to the community that they put together, we can't be quiet about exactly how that community is presenting itself to those outside of it. The squeaky wheel gets the grease.

If a group isn't being actively inclusive, it's being passively exclusive. This passive attitude results in lifestyle communities that do not reflect the local population. From the perspective of Philadelphia, where the population is 40+% white and 40+% black, you should expect to see an almost even amount of black and white people at local events. This has never been the case, in my experience. What *has* been the case, is finding myself as the sole person of color at mixers with dozens of attendees. What has also been the case, is being one of several people of color at a party…all of whom came to the party with me, or were invited by me and/or people who came with me. But I show up anyway.

It's exhausting at times, but I make it a point to be on-site as frequently as I can. Why? Because there is value in my visibility. People I've met at polyamory events have later told me, "I was kinda scared walking in, but I was so glad to see another black person there."

The ability to welcome, and make safe, other people of color in white spaces is something that I take seriously. It's something that I put aside my own social awkwardness to make possible. Outside of those spaces, I make it a point to engage with other polyamorous people of color both online and off. I often host movie-themed potlucks in my home. While these gatherings aren't usually connected to, or endorsed by, any particular local organization, they typically end up being far more diverse. I'm able to offer a comfortable environment to a wider range of people than most of the area events. My own tokenism provides room for other people of color who refuse to be tokens.

There is also a detriment to my tokenism. I understand this. While not quite the digital thievery of Diallo Shabazz's face, it is very possible that event coordinators can and will use my attendance as evidence that their social circle is diverse, inclusive, and welcoming. It's my body being used as proof. It's my image promoted as justification. It's for this reason that I'm rarely quiet about the topic of race and polyamory. Ummm…I wrote this book about it.

While I find there is value in my visibility in white spaces that are meant to be mainstream, I find there is more value in voicing how limited that visibility really is. It's obvious, laughable even, how individual I am at functions. It might even be easier, for organizers, for me not to attend. At least then they could pass off polyamory, locally, as something people of color just aren't into. But when I keep showing up, I serve as that elephant in the room. Everyone sees me, but nobody wants to talk about it.

I'll talk about it though. When I didn't like the way my marriage's image was used in *The New York Times Magazine* article, I almost immediately wrote a reaction piece to it. In my response, I voiced my dissatisfaction and explained exactly why I felt exploited by the experience.

I also appeared on the *Polyamory Weekly* podcast to discuss my expectations for the article and my frustration with its failings. I was not going to quietly let my name and face be used to promote an image of polyamory that was inconsistent with the reality or with my experiences.

This media-enforced inconsistent view of reality is frequently employed to excuse why polyamory groups and events can't seem to manage inclusivity. Organizers treat a lack of diversity as the standard, and not as a problem to be fixed…even if the tools are in place to make people of color feel more at home in mainstream groups. There are local meetups of groups like Black & Poly, and attendance at these functions fill the gap. All of the conspicuously absent people of color from the mainstream polyamory groups can find their numbers here.

So, if there are enough people of color at these meetups to meet the racial demographic percentages that the US Census figures claim are normal for a city like Philadelphia, why aren't these people of color attending events that are supposed to be mainstream?

FETISHIZATION

"It shows up in pretty much most of the messages that I get on my *FetLife* account. It's painfully clear that they haven't read my profile in any way, shape, or form. All they see is my picture. Their entire approach to me is, 'You're black! Can we do some race play? Can we do some slavery play? Can we do…?' a bunch of stuff that revolves around my race that I'm not interested in at all. Stuff that's clearly spelled out in my profile that I'm not interested in.

When I first started and I was doing more bottoming than anything, there were tops that felt that using racial slurs were OK in play. Or people would approach me for play or initiate a scene and then immediately try to take it to a racial place. Meanwhile, I'm thinking, 'We just met. You don't even know if I'm into that.' They just assumed that if I was black in a playspace that must be the reason I'm there. That's just not the case.

When I started topping more and doing more rope, I got the same thing, but in a different context. I was approached by lots of white submissives asking for me to dominate them in a certain way that fed into angry-black-woman stereotypes. As a result, I probably vet white partners way harder than I vet people of color. For me to get to the comfort level I need to play with someone who isn't black, they definitely have a higher bar to clear. I'm not going to put myself into a place where I'm vulnerable with someone who doesn't have my best interests at heart.

Of course, I'm vetting those black people as well. But the last thing I need is to be in a sub-space and immobilized when all of a sudden, this dude wants to play out his master-slave fantasies on my ass. Which is not what I agreed to."

– Scorpiana, Rope Bunny

In her popular series, *Tropes vs. Women in Video Games*, Anita Sarkeesian called out the poor treatment and representation that women received in games media. As part of her Feminist Frequency project, Sarkeesian shone a brutally honest spotlight on the oppressive nature of the games, the development, and the surrounding culture. In a video called *Ms. Male Character*, the critical eye was turned to some mid-level characters in the iconic Super Mario Brothers series.

"In the Mario franchise, the Koopalings were originally described as Bowser's seven children, all of them are male except for one, named 'Wendy O. Koopa.' We know she is female because her designers used practically every hyper-feminine frill and accessory available to separate her from her male siblings.

"Wendy's six brothers, by contrast, are 'unmarked' by gendered identifiers, which means they get to be presented in a variety of creative ways. Ludwig's design communicates intelligence and arrogance, while Lemmy's reveals his playfulness and Iggy's makes him seem maniacal and a little unbalanced. Sadly, Wendy's identity is limited by the fact that she is covered in superficial gendered signifiers. One look at her and you know she's female, but not much else. As with many Ms. Male Characters, her defining characteristic is her gender."

I bring all of this up because it is that same narrowing of identifiers that is the basis of fetishization. Onlookers take one look at you and limit you to a type that they can easily define, control, and interact with solely on their own terms. It's the same as othering with the addition of a sexual component. Instead of being seen as a human, those being racially or culturally fetishized become "a walk on the wild side" or an opportunity to add a new stamp to your ethnicity passport.

Obviously, this doesn't exist solely within a polyamorous context. It can occur in any setting where individuals or groups get together to celebrate, discuss, or seek out romantic partners. Being out and/or able to connect with other people in an alternative-lifestyle community is difficult enough, as is. There are always going to be longstanding social clues to stay aware of, in order to maintain one's personal safety. Being fetishized can make the newcomer to a social gathering feel like a sideshow. Life is hard enough when you have to deal with the oppressive conditions that plague people of color. It's tougher still when you're being treated like an exotic adventure by a crowd with whom you sought refuge. There is nothing welcoming about the notion that a positive reception, from a group or an individual, is based more on *what* you are than *who* you are.

It doesn't originate from a sexual context either. Fetishization is a product of the propagation of certain stereotypes. By definition, stereotypes are widely held but oversimplified images or ideas about particular types of people or things. Both fetishization and stereotypes have some basis in racist thought.

Some sexual stereotypes are based on singular experiences that just caught on...like a trend. In other cases, sexual stereotypes are the result of a culture being misunderstood by majority outsiders. Just as often, and historically, stereotypes appear solely for the purpose of demonizing or dehumanizing the people they are about.

Popular culture has reinforced every racial stereotype imaginable. They're all negative. Even the ones that sound positive act as a way to marginalize the people in a group who don't fit the mold. Also, it's not as if someone who places value on some seemingly flattering cliché, doesn't place equal value on a derogatory one about the same race. These stereotypes all come from a place of ignorance and short-sightedness. Limited exposure to people from different walks of life helps these outdated ideas stay relevant decades and centuries after their creation.

Along with the additional consequences that occur when people are poorly represented in media, stereotypes become a dominant source of information, factual or otherwise. Meaning, if you grow up with little direct contact with people of color, then it's possible that all you know is what pop culture shows you. If pop culture isn't getting it right, what are the chances that you will, in turn?

Pause for a second and think about it like this: How are Asian men commonly portrayed in media? Now, how are white men commonly portrayed in media? If you've got a significantly longer list of characters for white men, or if your list of Asian men still contains lots of roles that you're familiar with white men playing, it's only because you've been exposed to basically any type of medium available beyond the 19th century.

White characters are depicted as having a wide range of interests, hobbies, and abilities. People of color's characters are usually minimized, as far as what their characters "do," or where their characters "live." In many cases, people of color's characters are only included in lead roles because the narrative justifies their existence.

In video games, for example, Native-American lead roles almost solely exist because the protagonist absolutely has to be Native American. Either the main character is specifically dealing with Native-centric issues, or they have a skillset or character arc that's made up of stereotypical Native tropes, such as that of the "archer" or the "shaman." The only exception I've spotted is in the Sucker Punch–developed game *inFAMOUS: Second Son*. The protagonist, Delsin Rowe, is a member of a fictional Native group, but that only factors into where the man calls home. The other 98% of the story could be told about a person of almost any identity, without breaking the storyline.

When people of color don't receive that same "any person" treatment in media, it makes stereotypes seem like legitimate information about the unknown. This leads to people being seen as "rare" or "exotic," when really, they're just people.

It's a disservice both to the person who might just be trying to live their life, as well as to the person who genuinely wants to learn more about a culture they aren't a part of. Truly valuing something requires unpacking your hidden biases about that thing. This means understanding what is real, and what is just a tired misconception.

In any case, care should be taken to learn how these pop-culture influences and society driven biases affect the way we see people. None of us is left untouched by the society that we are born into. If it is unpalatable to you that your romantic approach may minimize humans into something "less than," it's worth examining the societal context that informed that approach. A person's humanity and sexuality isn't just fodder for someone else's entertainment. If your behavior or your interests indicate that you may feel this way, consciously or subconsciously, that is something that you can process and work through.

"I wouldn't necessarily say that everyone was having a good time and I wasn't involved. I think they definitely wanted me to be involved. But mainly in a sexual, black-plaything type of way. Pretty much every time I found myself in poly spaces it was like I was an object and not a person. It was really uncomfortable.

There's an adult play-lounge in our local area. They host polyamory events. In general, everybody who goes in there is open-minded and into different types of life-styles. Swinging and Polyamory and Kink. But all of those overlapping communities are predominantly white. So I've found that, with all of my interactions with white people in that lounge or in those kinds of events, I'm never treated as a person. Their attraction to me is always based in my blackness, or at least what they perceive blackness to be.

Through that, I can never really have an honest conversation. I'm in a place right now where I can't have any sexual or romantic interactions with white people. When I was at the start of my exploration, I was really open to it. Every single time that I reached out and went to a club or a meetup or something, there would always be some black angle towards my welcome into the group.

'We're so lucky to meet a black girl.' 'We don't get to meet too many black girls.' 'Come join this orgy!' 'Come be a part of our triad.' 'Come be with us because you're a black girl and that turns us on.' I can't even be specific about an individual situation, because they've all been so similar. None of them, in particular, even stand out to me."

– Alicia Bunyan-Sampson, Blogger

I've actually spent an evening at the adult play-lounge that was mentioned in the story. I was in town for a sex-ed summit, and the conference organizers were able to set up a discount door charge, at that same club, for anyone who arrived with an event badge. So a few of us attendees decided to make an appearance on the second night of the event. I went with four good friends.

The lounge was a well-run establishment. Going there when the location was packed with sex educators, adult-toy review bloggers, and human-sexuality students, meant that it was a really polite and consent-conscious crowd…for the most part. While engaging with one of the friends whom I arrived with — a white woman — I vaguely noticed people looking on.

As we were in an open location, there wasn't much that could be done. I honestly didn't give it much thought, in the moment. Especially seeing as how the onlookers didn't approach, interrupt, or even observe for very long.

No big deal, right?

Well, my friend left the club after that, accompanied by some of the others we came with. I stuck around a bit longer to continue socializing. The following morning, my friend told me that she had been harassed on her way out of the club. One of the onlookers from earlier had stopped her near the door. This man was not with our group of friends, and he was not one of the conference attendees. He appeared to be a regular customer at that club.

"Hey…I saw you upstairs with that black guy. It was really hot! I love interracial porn!" At this point, he attempted to inappropriately grab my friend. She knocked his hand away, and left with the rest of the group. Even at a swinger club — or should I say *especially* at a swinger club — consent and etiquette are a requirement. This guy's behavior, trying to grab my friend, was extremely shitty, and if the club staff had noticed, those actions should've gotten that guy removed from the venue.

An interesting aspect of that interaction was that this guy thought that fetishizing her playtime with me was the way to get my friend to engage with him, as well. He assumed that casting us as the lead roles in his fantasies was the way to make that fantasy come true. Even without the attempted assault, it's as insulting in a play-lounge as it is anywhere else in life. Up to, and including, your local polyamory happy hour.

Herein lies an additional bit of nuance that fetishization presents: There are people who believe they are being positive and complimentary in their fetishization. And it's hard to tell someone that they are being racially harmful when they are using certain behavior to get nearer to a person of color…as opposed to the flat-out racists who use harmful behavior to cause direct pain.

Don't get me wrong; I'm not trying to shame anyone for being sexual with their polyamory, or even from using sexuality to express themselves or their desires. But, you've got to pick your spots and make sure that you aren't alienating the very people you're trying to engage with. There are countless stories of racist microaggressions that are passed off by way of sexual interest. Through conversations about this very topic, I've heard more variations of the phrase, "I've never been with a black girl before" than I can count.

So, your admission to having "yellow fever" is not likely to be warmly received. And I've never looked at a flirtation as positive, when someone I've just met makes a pass at me that involves the initials "BBC," unless they were referencing news networks of the United Kingdom, which is something that's never happened.

Online dating profiles should not have to include disclaimers warning against the uses of terms like "caramel" or "cinnamon" or...ahem..."chocolate starfish." Seriously, there are ways to be sexual without being simultaneously oppressive.

It really shouldn't be hard to understand that it's not seen as a compliment to be a part of your sexual bucket list. Objectification is neither acceptance nor appreciation. Unpacking that basic idea is the first step in building meaningful relationships without being racially insensitive.

CLASS...

"Now my wife, Jane, and I live in Burlington, Vermont. A few blocks away from where we live, there's a very nice grocery store...supermarket. We buy good quality food, produce at a reasonable price. You don't have that here. So, the prices that people in this community are paying are substantially higher than what I pay. And the quality of the food that I get is significantly better.

I put my money into a bank. I get some interest rates. If I have to cash a check, I'm not paying 15, 20, or 50% or whatever the interest rate is to cash a check...because I have a bank. I didn't notice too many local branch banks in this community. Because I guess there aren't any. OK?

I can own a home, and at the end of the day you gain wealth when you own a home, and you don't have to rent. So, the truth of the matter is that the interest rates that poor people pay are often higher, they're paying rent rather than living in their own homes.

Not to mention that the jobs they're working in, by definition, are paying wages that are often inadequate to feed and to take care of their families.

So, being poor is, in fact, a very expensive proposition..."

– Vermont Senator, and then-United States Presidential Candidate Bernie Sanders, speaking in Baltimore about why it is expensive to be poor

In April of 2014, then-owner of the Los Angeles Clippers of the National Basketball Association, Donald Sterling, was revealed to have made egregiously racist statements to V. Stiviano, a girlfriend of his. Stiviano, who was involved in a legal dispute with Sterling's wife, Shelly, recorded him as he chastised her for associating with black people, including some notable professional athletes. Once these recordings were made public, there was a major outcry from those in the NBA community.

Everyone, from retired players, to current players, all the way up to the newly hired league commissioner, Adam Silver, had some level of harsh reaction. There were threats of player-led boycotts, a sort of wishy-washy protest from Sterling's own team, and strong pressure for an owner-led vote to remove Sterling completely from the NBA.

In the end, it was decided by Silver that Donald and Shelly Sterling would be forced to sell ownership of the team and that Donald would be held to a lifetime ban from the league. The team, which Sterling purchased for $12.5 million in 1981 and was then-valued at $500 million, would eventually be sold to former Microsoft CEO, Steve Ballmer, for $2 billion.

OK. Cool story.

Let me say this again in a different way.

A way that both highlights and simplifies.

A billionaire said some racist things that were caught on tape. In the process, he insulted some millionaires, which made many other millionaires upset. His millionaire employees threatened to stop generating money for their racist boss, but didn't. His fellow billionaires were concerned about the bad light that this situation was casting on them, and on their multi-billion-dollar product, so they threatened to push him out of their super-rich guy club. In the end, the racist billionaire sold his team to another billionaire, in exchange for more billions.

The end.

While the story, when told in full, is a bit more complicated than that, there's a huge chunk that's almost universally missing from the narrative of the Clippers' change in ownership. When this news broke, there was a massive response from the court of public opinion about the racist words Donald Sterling had said in V. Stiviano's recording. What was left mostly untouched was a response to Donald Sterling's long list of racist words and actions that spanned the decades preceding the events that led to his selling of the Clippers.

Had anyone bothered to run a *Google* search of Donald Sterling the day before the 2014 scandal broke, they'd have found several articles, public records, personal accounts, and lawsuits indicating a very long history of discriminatory practices. These alleged transgressions span far beyond the world of professional basketball, and are particularly centered around the areas of housing and employment. Housing and employment are possibly the two most important building blocks to increasing wealth and establishing a livelihood. In regards to people of color, Donald Sterling was known to get in the way of both.

A lot of people had hurt feelings over Sterling's offensive statements. A lot of rich and wealthy people were involved in removing him from his "billionaire boys' club." Those same people ignored the fact that he had been accused of specifically denying growth opportunities to people of color for decades.

Remember when I mentioned systemic oppression earlier? This is what it's built on: Limiting the means that people have to create a life for themselves based on some arbitrary aspect of their being.

Not to say that his statements shouldn't have been met with a harsh reaction. They should have. Not to say that they shouldn't have gotten him kicked out of the NBA. They should have. But it shouldn't have taken an adverse affect on a multi-billion-dollar product, or the bottom lines of rich players and executives, before anyone noticed what kind of man Donald Sterling was.

The problem here wasn't racism.

The problem here was money.

The problem here was class.

If this was about racism, more attention would've been paid to the actual practice of oppressing countless, non-famous, non-wealthy people of color, who were just trying to advance their own lives. In the same vein, more attention should currently be paid to the countless, nameless employers and landlords who have historically marginalized people of color basically since the *Emancipation Proclamation.*

A very specific practice among banks and real estate agencies was to block investment into certain areas. By denying loans to businesses that could raise the value and viability of a neighborhood, that area would quickly go underdeveloped. When local businesses went under, other businesses were deterred from replacing the failed ones. This would do tremendous damage to the community, as well as the local residents. Lenders would also deny mortgage loans to people of color who intended on living in higher-class areas, even when they were eligible and qualified to do so.

Instead, these consumers would be guided toward home ownership in the aforementioned underdeveloped neighborhoods, often at higher price points. The loans for higher-class locations and better interest rates would go solely to white customers, even those who were less-qualified or barely eligible.

This process was known as "redlining," due to the lenders' practice of outlining sections on a map, in red pen, to denote which sections of their coverage area were being targeted. An added detriment to these areas was the fact that many states fund their public schools through the use of property taxes, as opposed to state funding. So, in areas of huge financial disparity, a similar divide opens up between the education levels of those in well-to-do areas, and those who are living in poverty-stricken areas. When the red lines were being drawn, it affected the people within the lines and outside of them and throughout every aspect of their lives.

This is exactly the brand of marginalization that creates ghettos. It's the way class structures are enforced. The effects of these practices don't wash away easily, even after the practices themselves have ended. The effects stack up and become generational. It's the way finances and lodging become barriers for entry, when looking for love by way of polyamory.

"This has definitely come up lately, for me, with the conferences. There's a lot of discussion, especially recently, about diversity. But there hasn't been much going on, as far as accessibility. Last year, I was supposed to go and speak at the *National Sex Ed Conference* in New Jersey. I was all set to go. I had gotten a scholarship and everything. But, I ended up not being able to go because I was too busy being evicted. Because I didn't have money on my side, there was nothing I could do about it. It was bad in a lot of ways.

I had to go into a hotel. The money that I had been saving up went towards survival, at that point. I wasn't going to be able to travel and I wasn't able to do childcare or anything. I was going to have to step back.

There was another conference that I was invited to, *ConvergeCon* in Vancouver. The organizer personally reached out to me to let me know about it. But, just because I was dealing with everything, I ended up

not getting in my submission on time. So, that's
something else I missed out on because of money.

I like to say that being poor, every day is an emergency
basically. Everything you deal with is life or death. Constant
stressors. So, you miss a lot of things. A lot of opportunities.

I don't even know where I'm going to be in April
when that conference starts. Even if they had decided to
make an exception for my strained circumstances, about
all I have is my passport. Legally, I'd be able to go. But,
everything else, as far as travel, would still be in the way.

So, I'm literally missing opportunities because of
these kinds of barriers and the ways these systems
work. Where, if I want to go, I have to basically go
and do the impossible. If that makes sense.

It's a big reason why I'm excited about the
conference that I'm working on, because everyone
can stay the fuck at home. We don't have to worry
about accessibility for people with disabilities or
people with kids. We'll be able to work around it."

- Michón Neal of *Postmodern Woman*

According to the 2015 United States Census Bureau, the yearly
median household income is almost $20,000 lower for black
Americans vs. the average. It's nearly $25,000 lower vs. white
Americans. Combine that income disparity with the cumula-
tive effects of discriminatory housing practices, and it creates
a survival-driven, needs-based culture. It doesn't leave a lot
of time, energy, or resources for luxuries, and polyamory is
definitely a luxury.

A few things that polyamory thrives on are energy, time,
and emotional bandwidth. There are a lot of moving parts
involved in discovering, exploring, and expanding a relationship...let alone, multiple relationships. Each partnership
requires a certain amount of communication to establish

compatibility, to co-create boundaries, to set expectations, to build trust, and ultimately to define a structure with which to house other partnerships. Then you start the process all over again with someone else, assuming you're able to find other partners who are interested in inhabiting that structure you defined earlier.

So, when do you engage in all that valuable relationship-affirming communication? In the limited space between your full-time, minimum-wage shift, and your part-time, mini-mum wage shift? Do you find time on the phone, while taking public transportation to pick your children up from school or daycare? Do you find the time after you get home from wash-ing dishes...but before you have to write a paper for one class and study for an exam in another?

Do you see the problem here?

Whether we are talking about time or money or both, dat-ing can be expensive. Polyamory conferences can be expensive. Meetups can be expensive. Events centered around polyamory aren't always child-friendly, and babysitting can be expensive.

While all of this could be said of any luxury, the social nature of polyamory makes it particularly noteworthy. Polyamory communities can become awfully small and tight-knit over time depending on who is dating who. Missing events that you can't afford can be isolating.

In order to achieve maximum range to underrepresented people, Michón Neal and colleagues Jess Mahler, Louisa Leontiades, and Cassandra J. Perry founded the *Accessible Multi-linking and Polyamory Conference* in 2017.

Neal's conference takes place entirely online. For a group of organizers who specialize in concepts of financial distress, disabilities, and chronic pain, this conference is a creative solution to address all of these challenges at once. All of this occurs in an event that prioritizes co-creating intimate con-nections, while centering the voices of traditionally margin-alized populations. Having spaces that openly communicate about and make accommodations for class allows access for those who typically have a restricted path.

Depending on the way your polyamory is structured, the ability to bring a romantic interest to your home may also be a sticking point. For example, my wife and I live in a home that's large enough to comfortably fit multiple partners without very much forced interaction. While there's a fair amount of metamour love amongst my partners, part of this is contingent on the maintenance of each individual's personal space. If my family could only afford a small apartment, a lot of that harmony would immediately turn into friction.

Logistically, it takes spare resources to make polyamory function. Time. Lodging. Disposable income. It stands to reason that communities that have been generationally, often intentionally, left on the short end of the stick, will have trouble keeping up with polyamory's version of the "Joneses."

Although class, in American society, often breaks along racial lines, the two constructs face dissimilar difficulties when brought to discussion. Growing up, my mother would constantly tell me to eat all of my food because there were starving children in Africa. As I got to college, I learned that this was a common saying among lots of parents of picky eaters. It was a basic way of saying, "Don't take what you've got for granted. Cherish what you have because someone, somewhere has it worse."

The fact is, someone, somewhere always has it worse. So, why is class so easy to use as a casual admonishment towards stubborn kids, but so difficult to acknowledge as a barrier for entry to life's most basic comforts? Is it because the former is an abstract, featuring people from a far-off land, while the latter is much closer to home? I mean, it's not as if there aren't starving children all over America. I've never heard a parent tell their child to eat up because there are starving children on the other side of town. Maybe because it's harder to justify not feeding those starving children yourself, if they're in Africa.

Filmmaker Jamie Johnson is heir to a fortune. His great grandfather founded the *Johnson & Johnson* line of consumer and pharmaceutical products. Starting with his first film, *Born Rich,* Johnson is known for examining class from the perspective of the supremely wealthy. He was featured in the storytelling series *The Moth,* where he described some of the difficulties he faced after releasing that first film.

Aside from facing conflicts with friends, some of whom appeared in the film, Johnson was set at odds with his own father. The source of their disagreement was the long-held idea, among the rich, that the topics of money and class were both out of bounds. The implication here was that calling attention to class issues was a conflict of interest. Acknowledging the disparities worked against the systems that kept them in place.

Despite this conflict, Johnson stood behind his work and continued to create content that ruffled the feathers of the wealthy people he turned the camera on. His work could be seen as an effort to destabilize class oppression on a systemic level.

Now, unlike race or gender or sexuality, class is something that can be addressed on an individual level, which explains some of the unease in discussing it. I can recognize and buck against the societal conditions that enable my male privilege… but I can't hand any of that privilege over to those who don't have it.

A millionaire, on the other hand, can choose to immediately bring several people out of poverty. Of course, this doesn't create any manner of institutional repair, but knowing that you can but choose not to, can't be a fun place to be.

But class, as a factor of oppression, needs to be addressed and discussed for the same reason *all* of these barriers for entry need to be addressed and discussed.

If the goal is to improve conditions for yourself, your relationships, and your community, the first step is understanding your place in all of it… and owning your shit.

Fostering Inclusivity...
For White Folks

"...[I]t was the liberal answer to racism at the time. The thinking went that everyone should be judged by their personal talents and qualities, not skin color, skin color being irrelevant to intelligence, integrity, etc. If a person applied for a job, it was inappropriate to discuss their race in considering hiring them because that had led to discrimination in the past. Therefore, the thinking went, it was harmful to consider race *ever*. People should all be treated equally, even in the mind.

In many liberal households, this was very serious. Mentioning someone's race was considered oppressive, something no liberal parent wants their child to be. I was not allowed to use race to describe anyone, ever."

– Eileen Leslie of Central NJ Polyamory

So, if we're going to foster diversity in our polyamorous communities and in our social circles, we have to go straight to the source of what causes the divisions in the first place. If you thought this was just going to be a quick sheet of pro-tips to change the contrast of your groups and events...sorry. I mean, those tips are going to show up eventually. But, this process, first and foremost, requires introspection.

I want to tackle two things here.

The first is this idea of being "color blind," or saying that you don't "see" skin color, or race. This is harmful for a couple of reasons, but the most harmful aspect of it is that it's masked as harmless and tolerant and well-meaning. Instead, it's actually pretty dismissive. It ignores a lot of what makes us who we are. Cultural context is real. Shared lived experiences within a cultural context are real. We can't get away from this, nor should we. These aspects of who we are shape how we see the world around us. They should be respected...not dismissed.

I'm a dark-skinned man. I'm dark-skinned, and I'm a man. On a lovely summer day, I might walk outside and enjoy the sunshine. I've never worn sunscreen, and I ignore any suggestions that I should. Some of my lighter-skinned friends never leave the house without a bottle of sunscreen because they've dealt with sunburns ranging from irritating to severe. Sunburn is a non-factor in my life. It would be shitty and disingenuous of me to pretend that I don't notice that it's a factor in the lives of others.

On a lovely summer night, I might walk outside and enjoy the breeze. I don't worry about the length of my shorts or how much skin I'm showing. I wear whatever I feel like wearing. Although, I might catch a bit of flack from the neighborhood kids for dressing "like a dad," which I am, I never worry that my clothing might attract the attention of someone who might threaten my physical safety. Some of the women I know alter their clothing based on the area where they are traveling, for fear of such unwanted attention. Catcalling and uncomfortable sexual advances in public are non-factors in my life. It would be shitty and disingenuous of me to pretend that I don't notice that they are factors in the lives of others.

This is what being "color blind" does. The fear of having uncomfortable conversations about the world around us, allows us to simply ignore those uncomfortable conversations. It allows us to pretend that the shared lived experiences that define a culture aren't effecting and affecting people every day.

Again, "color blindness" can be really well-meaning. When someone says, "I don't see your race," what they are likely trying to say is "I treat everyone the same." On the surface, that sounds awesome. Once you add cultural context, though, the idea breaks down. When dealing with topics where a traditional, systemic imbalance is in place, treating people exactly the same dismisses the individual struggles that each person may face. Say I'm six-foot-four-inches tall. If you give me a foot-tall box to stand on, to see over a seven-foot-tall fence, awesome. I can see over the fence! If you give that same box to someone who's five-foot-four-inches tall, they are shit outta luck.

We need to address that a disadvantage exists here, and we need to work to remove that disadvantage for *everyone* before we can get to a place where treating everyone exactly the same produces a world of equality.

Look, it's all fun and games when we're talking about hypothetical boxes and fences. It becomes significantly less fun when the topic shifts to the way diversity presents itself in alternative lifestyle communities. Seriously, if it were all about being color blind, a single color wouldn't dominate in a statistically and demographically improbable way at local events and meetups. The fun and games go away completely when the topic shifts to imbalances in the way laws are written and enforced.

As a black man in America, I understand that anything from sitting on my porch, to walking through my neighborhood, has a statistically heightened chance of leading to a police encounter. A police encounter that has a higher probability of leading to my physical harm or to my death. That's a horrifying reality that I have to live with every day.

So, when someone tells me that they don't see color, what I hear is that my horrifying reality is too uncomfortable for them to acknowledge. That, because it's a non-factor in their life, they mean to be shitty and disingenuous by pretending not to notice that it's a factor in mine.

If you really want to be the positive force that you mean to be, by promoting color blindness, then acknowledge that boxes of varying heights will be necessary if we all mean to see over the fence. I'm not saying to pander to people of different cultures. Instead, *engage* with people of different cultures, find out what makes them unique, and try not to be a jerk about it as you learn.

Without acknowledging the variety of the human experience, all you get is the perspective of majority representation, which is mostly white and male and straight and able-bodied and cisgender and "traditionally" attractive. None of those things are inherently negative...but neither are their alternatives. So, all deserve some spotlight. All need to be recognized for their individual struggles and benefits...again, without being jerks about it.

Instead, respect and appreciate their unique circumstances and address any accommodations that stem from these differences. For me, this means keeping a tube of sunscreen in my car. I don't need it, but my lighter-skinned friends damn sure appreciate it.

"The first time I was assaulted, it was actually by the first person that I had sex with...ever. It was the summer that I turned 16, so I was just barely heading into my junior year of high school. He was a high-school senior.

It became this consistent push. He would come over to my parents' house and hang out. He would start with his hand on my knee, and I'd stop him. Then he'd have his hand on my thigh and I'd stop him. Consistently, over each time that we hung out, he would push my boundaries a little further with the attitude of, 'Well, you let me go that far before. Why won't you let me go a little bit further?' He kept guilting me into going in a direction that I didn't want to go.

At this point, I was super-religious and a member of an abstinence-only group. It was called 'Silver Ring Thing' and I had pledged to stay a virgin until marriage. They gave each of us a silver ring that had a biblical reference from First Thessalonians stamped on it. Something about abstaining from fornication and controlling your body and living in honor or some shit.

So, he kept on pushing and I would say 'no,' and he kept on pushing and I kept on saying 'no,' and then eventually we had sex…and I was not into it, and I was not happy with it, and I did not enjoy it because it was not what I wanted. I wanted to stay a virgin until marriage.

When I tried to talk to my friends about it, and tried to explain that I wasn't into it, and that I didn't want it, they treated me as if I just had buyer's remorse. One of my friends actually kidnapped my silver ring, and told me that I no longer deserved it because I was no longer a virgin. They didn't factor in that I didn't want any of this. They didn't treat me as someone who had suffered through an assault. To them, it wasn't rape, it was regret.

So, for a very long time, I didn't identify what had happened was any kind of violation of my consent. I was young but I had heard stories about rape. It was on TV and in movies. This wasn't some creepy stranger. This was someone that I went to school with. A guy that I invited over to my house. What happened to me didn't look like a *CSI* episode, and that's how my friends saw it. So, I accepted it. It wasn't until years later when someone pointed out that I had consistently given a boundary, and I was consistently pushed and coerced into going beyond those boundaries. I was never comfortable or happy with what happened, and the reaction of the friends who should've supported me didn't help. But that's when I understood that it was sexual assault."

– Rebecca Hiles, *The Frisky Fairy*

The second thing I want to get into is this myth of a "Big Bad." This idea of a pure, unquestioned, socially unacceptable source of harm that you can point to whenever harmful behavior is discussed, separating you from it. You hear it all the time when women discuss their personal experiences with rape culture and sexual assault.

A very common story you hear from women, involves a familiar acquaintance who pressured them into a sexual situation they were uncomfortable with. An exhausted "yes" that was bullied and coerced out of several incrementally weakened "nos." To which some guy, occasionally even that same familiar acquaintance, responds with something similar to, "I wouldn't call that sexual assault. It's not like I'm a weirdo in a trench coat who jumped out of the bushes, or dragged you into a dark alley or something. I was just being persistent."

Now let's leave off the problematic element of a person telling someone (especially someone that they violated) that their violation didn't really happen. *Google* the term "gaslighting" if you get some time though. The focus, for the moment, is the idea that sexual assault *looks* a certain way: A scary, trench-coat-wearing guy who snatches up unsuspecting strangers.

Although these types of assaults do exist, they are definitely in the minority. According to RAINN (Rape, Abuse & Incest National Network): Three out of four sexual assaults are perpetrated by people who are known to, or are intimately familiar with, the victim. So, if sexual assaults frequently occur like THIS, why do people only imagine it as THAT?

By pointing to "scary trench coat guy," one can absolve oneself of responsibility for perpetrating rape, or perpetuating rape culture because despite any character flaws you might have, or any behavioral missteps you might take, you can at least positively confirm that you're not THAT guy! That easy-to-recognize, universally hated symbol of all that is bad with the world.

The same occurs in the case of race and racism. The members of the Ku Klux Klan are racist. They are a hate group. It's kinda their thing, and it's been that way for just about all of ever. As far as racism goes, they are the Big Bad. So, when someone commits some racist microaggression, or blurts out a slur in a fit of anger, or declares that they just don't date people of color as a preference, they can reference the KKK as proof that they "don't have a racist bone in their body."

Despite any deep-seated prejudices that come out at inopportune moments, you can always whip out your wallet and display a complete lack of Ku Klux Klan membership cards. Thus, absolving yourself of any responsibility for furthering a culture that marginalizes people of color. Or, you can just point to your black friend...but more on that real soon.

The problematic element in absolving yourself of this example of the Big Bad, is that it closes the conversation without resolution. It silences the voices of the people who experience racism, and would like to see well-meaning, good-natured white people take up a larger role in fighting it. Also, and this should especially matter to white folks, it endangers those friendships with black people who you might have pointed out...but seriously, more on that in a moment.

"People aren't used to dealing with pain. In general, especially in the United States, a lot of it has to do with the lack of emphasis on emotional intelligence. Because people, as soon as they hurt, they want to heal. They want to get better. They're used to quick fixes. The quick fix belies the actual time it takes to heal safely and effectively. Most folks' idea of rectifying painful circumstances is denial and adrenaline, which results in more damage.

To confront these realities of oppression, people would have to literally question everything they've ever learned. They'd have to confront what they think the world is. So their foundation – who they are – a lot of that is built on unchecked privileges; to go through that takes a lot of work.

I don't think they'd want to deal with that pain, at all. Because it does hurt. So, we do get this kind of resistance.

We get a wall up where they end up rebounding on the people that bring up inequalities. They kill the messenger.

There is a lot of anger. They're angry at you for bringing this stuff up. Like, 'How dare you make me see this ugly thing? I don't want to look at it.'"

– Michón Neal of *Postmodern Woman*

The thing that makes systemic oppression so difficult to discuss is that when you do, you have to acknowledge your role in it. Often this means having to admit that you're part of the problem. It's not a comfortable experience when you learn that you further or benefit from the oppression of others.

At the beginning of this book, I listed a multifaceted series of privilege, which I am loaded with as a nature of my being. The first unearned advantage that I have, regardless of the type of privilege, is that I can ignore the issues that otherwise marginalized people experience. I can just decide that it's someone else's problem, I don't contribute to it at all, and no one can tell me otherwise...because I'll never have to face the consequence of my silence.

Ignoring the plight of transgender people in America will never make that plight mine. I'm a cisgender male. Presenting as male will never endanger my life simply as a result of someone finding me attractive. That's one of countless benefits that I have, that I need to remain aware of, and that I work to allow others to have. No one is asking for me to feel guilty for being cisgender, but I do have a responsibility to remain aware of what my gender affords me, and whether I need to use my privilege to amplify unheard voices.

If I tell you that I'm not transphobic, it's not because I got to the anti-transphobia finish line and now I can just rest there. If I tell you that I'm not transphobic, which is honestly not even an assessment that I can make for myself, it's because I try to work against a system that oppresses trans people in a way that leaves me untouched. It's because I listen to trans people and try to carry their words into spaces where I'm allowed entry and they are not. Sure, I can ignore it all…but I don't. I definitely don't get it all correct. I screw up, apologize, learn, and do better. There is no "finish line." It's an everyday thing for trans people. So, to some degree, I have to make it an everyday thing for me.

Race has to work the same way.

Point blank, you've got to own your shit! Own Your Shit!!!! You can't just point to your black friend and your lack of Ku Klux Klan membership and then sit silently in a world where racism is still an everyday struggle. You've got to acknowledge that race is a tough subject to discuss, and you've got to acknowledge that the source of that discomfort is white supremacy.

The source of that discomfort…is white supremacy.

This is a country founded on the broken bodies of people of color. A country built, and made rich, by the broken bodies of people of color. This stuff doesn't wash off in a generation or two — or even a century or two. It's an ongoing problem with lasting effects that touch *every aspect of society*. From the laws that govern our land, to the current membership roster of your local polyamory group, all the way down to your dating preferences.

But look on the bright side, we can all play a part in dismantling that system of oppression. The hardest part of that effort though, is admitting it's there, owning your part however big or small, and committing to using your voice, platform, and privilege in response. Unfortunately, guilt, defensiveness, and tears serve no real purpose in this process. You'll have to leave all of those behind…

…and in regards to your black friend, if you have indeed pointed in their direction, please stop. Just as we all need to divorce ourselves from the myth of the Big Bad, we also need to cast off the idea that having a person of color as a friend, lover, acquaintance, spouse, child, coworker, etc., is a way to prove that racism is someone else's problem. Seriously!

Misogynists have no problem dating, loving, marrying, or fucking women, all while remaining misogynists. The same is true with the issues surrounding race and racism.

Earlier in the book, I mentioned a Steph Guthrie tweet which read: "When you victim-blame, be aware that in all likelihood, at least one woman you know and love silently decides she cannot trust you." If I could rewrite that tweet in reference to people of color, it would be focused around the use of people of color as shields. Believe me when I say that that black friend feels the same way, and is making those same decisions, when they find themselves used as a defense against an accusation of real or imagined racism.

Unlike projecting the voices of people of color in over-whelmingly white spaces, waving your black friend as an anti-racism flag is the wrong way to invoke your friendship with a person of color.

It functions the opposite way.

In one case, you're saving your black friend from the emotional labor involved in educating groups of white people about race issues. In the other case, you're burdening that friend with the task of protecting you, while possibly working against their own identity politics.

The better tactic, instead of forming a defense, would be to listen and understand where the accusation is coming from and make adjustments as necessary. This way, you don't have to make it anyone's problem but your own.

Having had my own friendships mentioned as a security screen, of sorts, I can tell you that it's not easy…especially in cases where I disagreed with someone who I was invested in staying friends with. Now, I've got to defend someone who has exhibited behavior I would condemn in others. Now, I've got to say, "Come on, y'all. He's a good guy," to people who are feeling the same pain that I'm all too familiar with. Now, I've got to weigh the value of one friendship against that of others, with respect for my personal identity as the scale.

None of this should be the responsibility of that black friend, and it's shitty to hamper someone with this at the implied threat of a friendship lost. Seriously...just own your fucking shit!

DON'T PANDER...ENGAGE

"When we set up Atlanta Polyamory, Inc., back in 2010, it was as a meetup group. We did as much outreach as we could. Being that our leadership was cisgender and mostly straight in that group, we weren't able to attract, and even relate to, all the communities that we wanted to serve.

They said we were leaving them out...because we didn't know what we were doing. We didn't know how to go into those communities and do the outreach. So, when we decided to start the Relationship Equality Foundation to take over the *Atlanta Poly Weekend Conference*, we had some members that had been very active in the group.

One of them happened to be a genderfluid person, who was really tied-in heavily with the queer community. They had been bringing us a lot of the complaints, about our inclusivity, that came from that direction. So, we said, 'Well, if you're interested in taking over the group.' But they couldn't take the job at the moment, due to being too busy.

So, we found someone else to take over the group, and we almost lost the group entirely. They really did not have the skill set required to lead the group in a growing direction. Then our first choice became more available and they were able to jump in and lead a second takeover of the group. Now, it's really

flourished in that space. That community feels represented. So, it took a change of leadership to include
people who had knowledge of that community."

– Billy Holder of the Relationship
Equality Foundation

At the start of this book, I gave a quick analogy regarding the
difference between individual occurrences of prejudice and
systemic oppression. I wanted to be clear about this, because
of what happens when people confuse the two. When that
false equivalency gets made, almost invariably, oppressed people get pushed out of the discussion, and their legitimate complaints about a forced second-class citizenry, get trivialized by
those who once experienced a bad day. The conversation gets
watered-down and generalized in a way that ultimately helps
no one, especially those who need it most.

So, when a black character on the popular Netflix series
Orange Is the New Black remarked that the term "racism" could
be applied equally, I was frustrated. It isn't just because racism
was being downplayed by a black character in a fictional prison,
staffed almost entirely with white administrators. I understand
that black folks aren't a monolith and I've definitely heard people of color express similar views. It's also not just because that
character, Black Cindy, is nicknamed and identified by her race,
even amongst the black women who make up her core group
of friends. (I mean, seriously, you'd expect her black friends to
simply refer to her as Cindy when not in mixed company.)

My frustration came from the knowledge that the writer
of that line in the script was almost certainly white. Despite
having one of the most racially diverse casts on television,
Orange Is the New Black has a writing staff that is one of the
least racially diverse. In June of 2016, *Fusion* reported that of
the 18 writers who worked on the show during all of its then
four seasons, 16 of them are white. None of them are black.

So, for me, it felt like Cindy was less of a character in that moment, and more of a conduit for that same tired false equivalency promoted by the same people who benefit most from its propagation.

It's entirely possible that a black staff writer would've written similar dialogue for Cindy in that scene. It's entirely possible that a black staff writer would've given a thumbs-up to that dialogue during a read-through for that episode. But, it's also entirely possible that a black staff writer would've heard the lines and objected to them as far too problematic for a savvy character like Cindy.

Without any black writers in that room, we'll never know.

The people with the power to shape the narrative, do exactly that, from their own points of view. An all-white writers' room can't always be expected to properly capture the perspectives of a racially inclusive cast. Just as an all-white group of organizers for a polyamory meetup face the same limitations.

In any alternative lifestyle communities, when the question of inclusivity comes up, the first response should be an examination of, or a discussion with, those with the potential to affect change.

Maybe the people in charge don't realize there's an issue, or maybe they just aren't qualified to solve it on their own. In either case, more hands are needed to help sort things out. The addition of people of color in guidance roles can alter the landscape of the group's demographic. Outreach-wise, a change in leadership can bring your polyamory group into closer contact with communities that are being underrepresented. New viewpoints can also expose blind spots in event planning.

Even outside of logistics, a change in leadership can equal a change in optics. Obviously, the difference needs to be about more than just visuals. Proactive steps need to be taken, as well. But it can't be discounted just how comfortable people can be made to feel when they spot someone who looks like them at an event that they've been told is for others. A new face for your group can be the signal of a new direction.

On the occasion that someone calls out my blog, *Poly Role Models,* for not being inclusive to a certain community, my first response is to invite them to be a part of the process. Either I ask that person if they'd like to be a contributor to my blog, or if they know of others who may be willing to share their stories with my readership.

I recognize that I can only do responsible and effective outreach to so many communities. So, I hand over the reins to those who can see my blind spots better than I can.

Addressing the concerns of other polyamory-friendly communities can function similarly. Who is complaining about the lack of inclusivity? Are they in a position where they can be a part of the solution? If not, do they know someone who *is* willing? These are the questions that need to be considered.

I understand that moving around leadership isn't always easy, especially if you are part of that leadership. There is a lot that comes into play, and not everyone wants to take their hands off the steering wheel. But part of leadership is looking at the goals you want to accomplish, and putting the pieces in place to make those goals happen. Even if that means occasionally moving yourself off the board.

INTENTIONAL PLANNING

"I think one of the pivotal things we did, was having monthly group planning meetings from the get-go. So, we always opened up a space to our members to come and speak. We took various members' opinions and brought them to that table, even if they couldn't attend. There were many voices at the table. They weren't always as diverse as I would've wanted them to be, but we tried to seek them out as best we could.

I certainly came from the standpoint of being on an LGBT platform and from an Indigenous background. So, I always tried to highlight those types of areas and I was very aware of who we needed to take into consideration.

What accessibility concerns were there? Not just physical accessibility, either. Right away, when people hear 'is it an accessible space?' They think 'wheelchair accessible.' But it's also about sound and light and smells. And then cost! Can it be accessible by cost?

I've tried, as often as possible, to have our events be free or very low-cost. Like by donation or pay-what-you-can. That really seemed to help out with our community. What you actually find, when you leave the room open for pay-what-you-can, is that you get a lot more than you expected.

So, in addition to that, what helped was just really opening up the platform and allowing ourselves to be told that we didn't do something quite as right as we wanted to. Listening to the feedback from the community. Getting into an event space and asking ourselves, 'Are the people here that we want to see?' If they're not, 'Why are they not here?'

If we want to have purposefully inclusive events, we have to look at where we are advertising. Although we feed everybody back to our meetup group, we still do advertising in other ways. The 519 Community Centre is the hub of the LGBT community. Our name is frequently up on their scheduling board. People regularly pop into our events and ask what polyamory is all about. So, we can do lots of cross-community promoting, just by word of mouth. Just by being in the right place. Being in the right venue."

– Eva Dusome of Polyamory Toronto

So, you don't know why you can't draw a more diverse crowd to your monthly happy hour. Your Polyamory 101 discussion group is full of the old familiar faces, but not the newer crowd that would benefit from learning the basics? Well, let's act like you skipped over the last bit of this book, which was about switching up your organizers. Let's jump to the events themselves. As I've said before, if you have an exclusive-appearing crowd, it's not a coincidence. So, changing this can't be a coincidence either. You can't just hang up a "Welcome" sign and expect diversity to occur on its own. You've got to make inclusivity an intention and not a happenstance.

Now, I'm gonna ask you a bunch of questions, feel free to answer them in your head.

Are your events intentionally planned to draw the most inclusive crowds?

Where are you hosting your get-togethers? Meaning, what parts of town?

If your local area is segmented by way of race, it makes sense to counteract that while planning a meetup. Maybe there's a downtown location available that can serve as a halfway point for the crowds you're intending to draw. If it's not a centralized location, maybe it can be an alternating one.

Can your group host multiple events to accommodate different communities?

What types of events are you hosting?

Which types of activities are available?

What types of venues are you considering? Maybe Saturday night at a kink-friendly playspace, Sunday morning brunch at a high-end restaurant, and Tuesday night bowling at the most popular lanes in town, which means all of these potential events might attract different crowds of different races, ages, and disability statuses.

It's up to the organizers to figure out how well their events are received by the people they are trying to reach out to.

Contemplating the parental responsibilities of your intended guests is another facet of intentional planning. That brunch or that bowling night could be reasonable events to bring children to. Saturday at a swinger club, though, might require parents to arrange for a babysitter, which is yet another expense that guests would have to consider. So, another factor that organizers should also have to consider.

Now, if class is a barrier for entry, how are you staying mindful of the costs? Hosting a get-together at a bar or restaurant may price-out some of the people who would've liked to attend.

What ends up being more important to your group's goals? Is it the population and its demographic, or the ability to host your gathering at a particular venue?

Conferences often have tiered-pricing structures that adjust for differing levels of household income. Polyamory Toronto is known to ask attendees for "pay-what-you-can" donations, or flat-rate contributions of toonies (two-dollar coins). Some communities are large enough or well-resourced enough to be able to hold events for free.

A staple of many polyamory groups is the potluck. Simply put, it's a party where guests bring food with them. Each year, I host several potlucks in my home. Unfortunately these events create a different problem. Although they are both family friendly and free to attend, parties at my home are outside of the local metropolitan area. Thus, they aren't as easy to reach by mass transit. I can't exactly move my home to accommodate the occasional potluck but, at the same time, I do try to offer rides to nearby train stations and bus stops to accommodate anyone wishing to attend. While my home may have this specific limitation, the parties that I host are not typically attached to any particular local polyamory group.

Events that *are* hosted by a local group should be available and accessible to the whole community. If public transportation is an option, venues should be chosen to minimize the distance from transit stops. Locations should be accessible to persons with physical disabilities, and accommodating to people with reported sensitivities to light, sound, smell, or cigarette smoke.

All in all, intentional planning is about examining the needs of those you mean to serve and rising to the occasion. It's not always going to be easy, but it doesn't have to be hard. Organizers can add membership and delegate responsibilities. They just have to remember to maintain a committed and receptive approach to hearing people's concerns, and addressing them whenever possible.

JOINT EVENTS

You might've picked up on it, due to some of the references that I've used in this book, but I'm a geek. I spend my free time playing video games, watching science fiction, and reading comic books. A favorite element of mine in comic books, is the "crossover special." If you're unfamiliar with the concept, crossovers are when two, normally separate comics merge into a joint storyline.

When crossover specials are published, fans of each series check-in because the book they love is involved. So, they don't have to feel uncomfortable with unknown characters, because the ones they're most familiar with are right there in the mix. Not only are their favorites there, but fans get to see them interact in ways they typically wouldn't. For instance, the loner from the *X-Men* finds a kindred spirit on the *WildCATS*. The unique talents of the *Justice League* end up being the final piece of the puzzle in helping the *Avengers* defeat a brand new foe. Characters mix-and-match characteristics in unusual ways, and then they depart as friends.

Joint event-planning can be managed in the same way. By reaching out to other local groups to host activities together, several goals can be accomplished at once. Two polyamory groups, serving two different populations, can reach a greater number of members. They can also pool their resources to make the event itself stronger. Most importantly, the groups can offer one another new perspective on what type of venture to undertake in the first place.

Polyamory groups that are intentional communities, like Black & Poly, exist all over the country. Having a joint commitment from a group that serves a particular community presents the opportunity for a more-mainstream group to see an increase in diversity.

At the same time, members of that intentional community will be assured that they won't be going to an event that might leave them isolated. It's a win-win.

Aside from attendance numbers, advertising range also increases. Two groups might not host or broadcast their parties in the same places, but with a joint party, they have the opportunity to do exactly that. The benefits don't need to be a singular occurrence, either. I've never heard of a polyamory group that barred its membership from being affiliated with other polyamory groups. Finding fellowship, through joint events, can create lasting inroads, more intuitive inclusivity, and a stronger global community.

Basically, a rising tide lifts all boats. So, reach out, make friends, and form networks. Kinda like polyamory in general.

Fostering Inclusivity... For People of Color

SHOW UP...OR DON'T...

"As I recall, somebody posted in the *Queer Exchange*, which is a very active group. They asked if anybody knew any groups or social outlets for people who are some kind of non-monogamous. They didn't specify polyamory, but they were looking for groups that had strong abuse and anti-predator protection practices, and are also very queer-friendly and welcoming. That was the initial post.

There were lots of responses. I don't remember which happened first, but a couple of people shouted out the local polyamory group, and then a couple of other people said, 'I don't recommend that group either as being a safe space for survivors, or as a particularly safe space for queer people.' So then, obviously, there was a lot of discussion.

Many, many people chimed in on that comment, to agree that they weren't doing a great job with that. Even when people asked about recent policy changes, something that I had more specific knowledge of, I brought up that their policy changes haven't been reflected in their practice or behaviors yet.

Since then, I have been happy to see that the group has had some response. There have been some steps taken. I'm still withholding judgment or approval until I see how everything shakes out."

- Ginny Brown, Writer and Sexuality Educator

I've been lucky enough to be able to travel around North America to speak about polyamory. One of the joys that I get out of the experience are the head nods. Imposter syndrome is a real thing, and I always worry that I'm not as keyed-in as I think I am. But then I start talking about how race impacts polyamory, and the people of color looking on start nodding their heads, as if I was telling their stories rather than my own.

Turns out, I'm addressing a lot of our stories. That's the easiest way for me to recognize that racial imbalances in our communities and events aren't just my individual experience. I like to think, though, that by opening my mouth about these experiences, I can either alter the landscape or at least provide some solidarity for others who live it the same way I do. These two goals, specifically, alter the landscape and provide some solidarity.

This is why I show up.

Don't get me wrong, I also find fun and fellowship with my local groups, but part of my attendance is agenda-driven. I try to be that representation. Not for the group's demographic appearance, but for other people of color who might need to see my face. Since I know what it's like being the only person of color at a polyamory event, when new people of color show up, I try to make myself present in a way that still feels like natural interaction. Whether we get along, or not, whether we practice similar styles of polyamory, or not; I want my visibility to confer the idea that there is a place in this relationship-style for all of us.

Now, I just said, "There is a place *in this relationship-style*" because I don't want to vouch for any groups that I'm not an organizer for. Even if polyamory isn't just "white people's shit," the local community might still be, despite my visibility.

I've had experiences where I've befriended people of color at mainstream meetups, we've remained friends, they've come to parties at my home, they've showed up to Black & Poly events…but they've refused to return to the mainstream meetups where we met. Even if I was welcoming, they felt that the group was not.

There's a saying that I've used earlier in this book: The squeaky wheel gets the grease. For those who don't have the patience or desire to be uncomfortable, another option is to get loud from the sidelines. Instead of going to polyamory-centered events, just don't. But never hesitate to explain why.

Explain why in person.

Explain why on social media.

Explain why in spaces reserved for intersecting populations, like kink, burns, or swinging.

Alternative lifestyle communities can be really tight-knit, especially when they serve overlapping needs, and word often travels fast. Not just in your area, either. It only takes one far-reaching polycule or the right post in the right place, to turn your local business into common knowledge.

Now, my apologies if I gave the impression that these strategies are mutually exclusive. Just because you're showing up, doesn't mean you can't also get loud. In some cases, having close proximity, imparts a certain social cachet that a relative stranger might lack. At the same time, being a loud outsider doesn't mean that you can't provide solidarity. Using your voice effectively can be a beacon to others who soundlessly agree, but have been afraid to speak up.

So, show up...or don't. But, if you want to affect a change, do so with intention.

In both cases, whether showing up or staying home, please be mindful of your own well-being. Showing up to places where you aren't entirely comfortable takes a lot of emotional energy. No one should be expected to do this on regular basis, particularly if it's optional. Getting loud from a distance also takes its own toll. Alternative lifestyle communities can easily become victim to cults of personality. Calling out problems in a community or running afoul of the wrong popular organizer, even for the right reasons, can lead to a social backlash. There's always the risk of being labeled a "malcontent" and facing ostracization.

Take care of yourself in the way that makes the most sense for you. Create a circle of trusted friends who you can be yourself around. Schedule quiet alone time for yourself. Cultivate a hobby that you find fulfillment in. Get some exercise. Replace all of your socks. No one is expecting you or anyone else to be a 24/7 crusader for any cause. So prioritize your self-care. And when you're ready, get back at it.

YOUR EVENTS ARE YOURS

"I don't want people stuck with saying 'Oh, it's another potluck with another group.' I just try to get people out doing different things. I've tried to do *Painting with a Twist*. I might try it again. We've done dinner at Maggiano's. A woman from a polyamory group in Florida had reached out to me. She was in town and wondered if we could do dinner. My thought process was to do something that was easy for everyone and Maggiano's has a family style meal at a lower price. That was easy to put together.

I just try to think of different things that would interest people. We had a bowling night that went well. So, we'll have to try that again. For me, I just think about stuff that I'd like to do, and then see if others would like to do it, too.

I do try to make it [events] as centrally located as possible, so transportation won't really be an issue. I do try to find things that are moderately priced. The group dinner and the painting were relatively inexpensive. And you know we have a big family, so I try to give people enough notice as possible. So people can have the funds. You know things can be tight.

Even when we do barbecues in the summertime, if everyone pitches in, it's not as costly as it might be on one person. As far as the events that I try to put together, I try to do a variety of things. I try to do stuff for families or for just adults. A lot of times, people want to get away from the kids. Other times, it's good for kids in poly families to be around other kids in

poly families. Family events are attractive to people
as well. I definitely take all of it into consideration.

– Shallena Everitt, head of Black &
Poly: Philadelphia Chapter

If going to, or avoiding, events isn't really your thing, you can just start your own events. If it sounds simple, it's because it mostly is. The biggest barrier here is resources. Surprise!

But let's say you've got a surplus of money or time or emotional energy. You have enough of a surplus of these things that you want to spend that extra bit on yourself, and go on a nature hike. You can turn that hike into a polyamory event, just by inviting polyamorous people to hike with you. Just like that.

You can find polyamorous people, presumably for your hike, in any number of places. The magic of the Internet makes it straightforward. Every form of social media can be a tool for reaching people. That's why it's called "social" media. Ethical non-monogamy has more than one *Subreddit*. It has searchable hashtags on *Twitter, Tumblr*, and *Instagram*. *Facebook* has multiple groups, each with more than 10,000 users, who are focused on polyamory. *Meetup, Kasidie,* and *FetLife* all facilitate non-monogamous groups.

With the combined reach of these networks, you can cultivate the population of your choice. Creating a population simultaneously creates a resource pool. Lots of venues offer group discounts if you can bump up the headcount. Maybe an invitee can provide a quality tent to bring out for the hike. More people can be useful in this way. They can also be dubious. Wherever you go, whatever you do, make safety a top priority. Your personal safety, and that of anyone who turns up because they are effectively under your care.

Of course, there's also the option of extending your event to the community at-large. Assuming that the community at-large isn't generally unsafe, this may carry the benefit of having a better-vetted group of attendees. At minimum, you should have a wider variety of references, per attendee, regardless of how well they've been vetted by the larger community. This should allow you to select participants who you find agreeable to be around, and who you feel should take a hike…just not *your* particular hike.

Regardless of the type of people who appear interested in your hike, make sure you put your stamp on the event. Whether by the creativity of the activity, or the way it's presented, make it yours. Develop something you'd want to be invited to, and support the good times that follow. You might just find yourself as the go-to person for your kinds of events, or environments. So, when it's time to host a nature-amory hike, everybody knows who to call.

I don't know why I keep talking about hikes. I'm not outdoorsy at all. As I mentioned earlier, I actually host potlucks at my home. It's not terribly original, but they don't cost much time or effort to arrange. For me, the hardest part of planning the event is picking a theme, and sending the invitations. As far as themes go, it's usually about just selecting which kinds of movies I want to watch with friends. Bad movies? Christmas films? The collected works of Paul Verhoeven? Tough call. And invitations? They're not really hard, but I invariably forget to invite someone, and they invariably let me hear about it. That's about as fun as sounds.

MAKE YOUR OWN GROUP

"Phillip and I were looking to meet people. I kinda decided that I didn't want to be monogamous. That was where we started. I had done a lot of research online and I found out about polyamory. After that, we wanted to get involved in the community as much as we could.

We went to a couple of meetups, and both times we just felt like it wasn't really the place for us. It felt like there was a lot of sex-based stuff, and it also felt like there was a lot of processing. There wasn't a lot of community building or friendship building or like fun activities.

The first one that we went to was a group discussion. But everybody just wanted to ask us questions because we were new and interesting. It was a huge turn-off for us because we were there to learn more. We didn't want to be the ones talking. The second one? One of the people there ended up crying the whole time, and her partner was not very emotionally supportive of her. That whole thing was very uncomfortable.

At that point, I was like, 'I just want to sit around and eat food and chit-chat and have fun.' So, I threw a potluck and invited anybody I found on *OkCupid* who was self-described as polyamorous. That was pretty much the start of the group. There were 24 people, mostly couples.

After that, somebody said, 'Hey you should make this a *Facebook* group, so that we could all keep in touch and maybe do another poly-potluck.' At the time, it was something I was doing a lot of. So, it made sense for me to just keep throwing parties. Once we made the group, somebody offered the name, *Polydelphia*.

Everything just took off from there."

– Tiffany Adams, co-founder of Polydelphia

If a welcoming community doesn't exist, consider creating your own. The same motivation that drives the creation of a single event can be broadened into much more. The only thing you need to form an intentional community is recognition of a need for that community's existence. Whether we're talking about Black & Poly, Polydelphia, OpenSF, or Polyamory Toronto, somebody detected a demand, and constructed something to fill that void. The only thing that separates creating an event and creating a community is intentionality, or the deliberate purpose to form something that lasts longer than an isolated experience.

With a group of your own construction, you can set the terms and actively seek out the people who will most benefit from the need that you're addressing. The same social-media approach applies as when you're starting up an event.

The major difference is that a community implies a commitment to a goal, to center a voice or to serve a population or to accomplish a task. Communities typically have names and unifying principles.

So, make something that you can call your own, and prepare for it to grow. But another thing to remember is that, just like polyamory, affiliates of a group don't need to remain exclusive to that group. You can recruit membership from groups that address overlapping needs, without damaging them in the process. You can also create a cycle of pooled resources with and mutual respect for other communities. Or you can isolate yourself entirely. It's up to you.

But, in either case, be the recommendation for someone who is looking for a group like yours. As sugary as this may sound, something you create can be exactly what someone needs!

Speaking of creating something...

START CREATING

"Not too long after I started up the *Poly Role Models* blog, something pretty awesome happened. In a single turn of events, I had hit what I thought was a snag, then got slammed in the face with imposter syndrome, and then immediately gained the maximum amount of validation for the work I was doing.

In the first few months, my interview series was able to showcase the experiences of a few well-known sex educators and big-name polyamory-celebrities. I had gotten some critical notice, and a bit of media exposure that allowed my little labor of love to truly take off. But then I started getting worried that I didn't have enough content to go forward. Some of the wonderful and insightful people I had hoped to put in my blog, including the publishers of my race and polyamory book, hadn't answered any of my emails. Sure, I had the next couple of weeks covered, but what happens after that? I wanted to have a content surplus of several months.

Out of fear, I reached out to a friend of mine and asked her about appearing on the blog. There was a unique aspect to her polyamory that I was pretty impressed by. Not only was she a woman of color, not only was she the hinge of a mostly-exclusive V with two men of color; those two men were a pair of brothers who didn't always get along. At the time, despite a lot of friction, they were making it work. As far as I was concerned, any amount of success my friend had with this particular structure made her an American icon.

The problem, for me, was that I didn't reach out to my friend because of her quirky polyamorous dynamic. I reached out because I felt desperate. Although interesting to the point of noteworthiness, I didn't have any particular draw to the way my friend practiced her polyamory. Nothing against it. It just wasn't how I practiced my own. Add all that to the fact that she wasn't some educator, organizer, podcaster, or whoever else with a website and a brand to promote. My friend really stuck out in comparison to the other people I had already profiled on the blog. So, I was a little nervous when her appearance went live.

Less than an hour after I published my friend's profile and promoted it all over *Facebook*, I got a private message from someone pretty important. It was one of those big-name, polyamory-celebrities, who was the kind of person with a lot of charisma and influence and connections and stuff. They had read my friend's profile and they weren't all that impressed. As a measure of constructive criticism, they suggested that I should add some sort of intro to every profile to describe exactly why each Poly Role Model should be considered as such. It was a sort of disclaimer for why you should even bother reading the entry.

This suggestion was well-meaning and earnest, of course, but it kind of felt like a gut punch. Not because of the criticism itself, and definitely not because of the individual dishing it out, but because of what it might mean. It played into all of my fears about the validity of my blog's purpose. I posted a profile that I wasn't really sure about, and I immediately got called on it. It looked like I had run out of noteworthy names, and was just filling my blog with my pals. Now, everyone was going to figure out that I'm just an imposter. My work is fraudulent, I don't really belong here, I'm ugly, and my mother dresses me funny.

I wasn't going to tell this person that, though.

Instead, I freestyled an explanation that ended up being the absolute truth. I responded to the suggestion by clarifying that 'Every role model is a role model to whomever needs that role to be modeled. This profile doesn't need to resonate with the two of us. It's going to mean the world to someone else who really needs it.' I quickly navigated my way out of that conversation with that same feeling of having just dodged a punishment from my dad…but was still maybe on thin ice.

The magic happened less than twenty minutes later in a *Facebook* post that I was using to promote my blog. A woman, who was a user of this particular forum, posted a response gushing about the latest profile. This user absolutely loved the appearance, and was glad to see anyone speaking about being in a mostly exclusive V relationship with two brothers. My friend's polyamory was precisely how this user wanted to style her own polyamory. This profile was exactly what she needed in order to feel validated in her structural desires…and her post was exactly what I needed to feel validated in my work.

The big-name, polyamory-celebrity who had made the suggestion to me was a user in that same forum, and had recently posted in that same thread. So, I'm almost certain they saw this woman's response…and I'm more than certain that I spent the rest of that evening high-fiving myself.

Since then, I've paid much closer attention to the responses I've received for each *Poly Role Models* profile from the blog's readership. Not a week goes by when I don't see someone's thankful response that their identity has finally received some visibility in a polyamory-designated space. Now, I don't know if I'm ever going to feel like I'm not an imposter. But I absolutely do know that I've provided a platform that people are getting value out of. There's something really warm and fuzzy in the simplicity of that."

- Kevin Patterson, curator of *Poly Role Models*

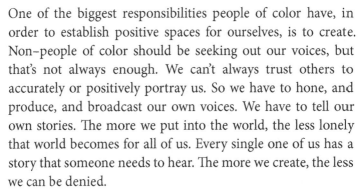

One of the biggest responsibilities people of color have, in order to establish positive spaces for ourselves, is to create. Non–people of color should be seeking out our voices, but that's not always enough. We can't always trust others to accurately or positively portray us. So we have to hone, and produce, and broadcast our own voices. We have to tell our own stories. The more we put into the world, the less lonely that world becomes for all of us. Every single one of us has a story that someone needs to hear. The more we create, the less we can be denied.

We won't all be ignored.

We can't all be ignored.

Now, as a heads-up among other examples, I'm about to cite my own blog all over this chapter. When I started doing workshops about race and polyamory, I came up with the list, you've already seen, of barriers for entry that people of color encounter in polyamorous spaces. I would be giving myself far too much credit if I claimed that I intentionally meant for my blog to address as many of those barriers for entry as it does. It's really just a reflection of what I wanted to see, as far as representation goes. So, seeing as how you're about to get quite familiar with its inner-workings, I might as well give you a brief rundown of how it got started.

HOW I STARTED CREATING...

I had made a huge screw-up.

My wife, Autumn, often takes some of the blame, but in my head the fault is mine. I had scheduled overlapping time with two fairly new partners. Charley was arriving to spend a week with me, and Tali had already established a routine of spending every other weekend at the home I share with my wife and kids. Everyone was sort of excited about the prospect of spending this much time together. Or so it seemed. Autumn was mostly quiet.

My wife can be distant at the best of times. But part of our dynamic is in me knowing when distant meant, "I want to be away from everything," and when it meant, "I want to be away from YOU." I tried to pretend that it was the former, but I knew it was definitely the latter. She was pissed. The time with Charley and Tali was pretty amazing...for the three of us. By Saturday though, when Charley left, I could tell that Autumn was completely done with having company. So by the time Tali went home on Sunday, I knew that a fight was about to happen. And it absolutely did.

Autumn and I had a big blowout. I hadn't been checking in on her needs. As I said, she can be distant. So, when I spent so much time bundled up with Charley and Tali, I didn't think Autumn would miss me. But, that was just a guess. A bad one. At the same time, Autumn hadn't actually voiced her concerns with me over the course of the week. She just silently steamed, waiting for me to pick up the hints. I didn't ask, she didn't tell, and then there we were, mad at each other.

We almost ended our relationship that day. Thankfully, we were able to own our parts of the problem. Somehow, we righted the ship by the end of that same argument and were happy with the new perspective the situation had given us.

The following month, at our local polyamory meetup, Autumn and I told the story of how badly everything had gone during that week. The group's organizer was shocked about it all. My wife and I almost always appear to be that couple that has it all together. For us to have gotten so close to the edge was a surprise. Equally surprising was how well we rebounded from such touchy circumstances. And that's when she said it…"You two have been doing this for so long! But you're still finding new ways to fail, process, and recover. It's like the two of you are poly role models!"

The car ride home was full of ideas! I latched onto the term "Poly Role Models" and annoyed the fuck out of my wife with all the concepts it inspired. I considered Brandon Stanton's photography blog, *Humans of New York*. I thought about the interview style of Aisha Tyler's *Girl on Guy* podcast, and particularly her spotlight on spectacular failure, *Self-Inflicted Wounds*.

These two projects would shape two of the most important functions of *Poly Role Models*: The awareness of imperfect, yet successful polyamory, and the inclusive representation in polyamory. A huge bonus to that second function was the eventual inclusion of the blog's eighth question. The question about each respondent's self-identities, and how those identities impact their polyamory, is easily the most popular and possibly the most important.

That bit took a few months to make real, but within a month of coming up with the concept, I had a functioning blog that was a "free resource" for anyone who wanted to enjoy it.

CREATING AROUND CLASS…

Now, the term "free resource" is a bit tricky. So, I want to take a moment to acknowledge this leading into discussing the barrier of class. The fact is, there is no such thing as a "free resource." If it takes time to create, time to observe, or time to consume, that's time and energy that you're not spending putting money in your pocket. Many of the assets that we take for granted as "free," have a financial cost that we don't attribute to the asset itself because it's a cost we would've paid regardless of our need for that asset.

So, when I use the term "free resource," I mean to describe any resource or material that does not have a specific additional dollar amount beyond your ability to access that resource.

For example, *YouTube,* as a website and as a mobile application, is free to use. Unfortunately, it requires Internet access and Internet-accessing technology, both of which typically cost money. By this standard, *YouTube* costs money. But, if you already intended on having, say, a smartphone in your pocket and WiFi in your home for reasons unrelated to your use of *YouTube*, then I consider *YouTube* to be a free resource.

Another free resource? The ability to walk into an Apple Store.

When his home computer crashed, then 25-year-old rapper Prince Harvey made do by using his local Apple Store as a functional recording studio. He believed in his own work so much, that he wouldn't let any technical difficulties deter him from creating.

Harvey would show up every weekday, for four months, to record his acapellas on the store's display-model computers. He utilized the store's resources, including some human resources in the form of some understanding Apple Store employees, in order to produce his art. What he couldn't hide on the computer's hard drives, he would smuggle out by way of emails, and a portable thumbdrive. In July of 2015, Prince Harvey was able to release, as a completed composition, an album called *PHATASS*...meaning Prince Harvey At The Apple Store: Soho, which is possibly the most relevant album title in hip-hop history.

When I began creating, I decided to utilize only free resources. This was a labor-of-love, and something that had potential I didn't quite understand. I didn't want to spend any money that I knew I wouldn't be getting back. At the same time, I didn't think that charging money for this new idea would've gotten me very far. So, I never stopped to think of ways to really monetize the content I was providing.

In discussing all of the possibilities with my partners, I settled on *Tumblr* as the best possible outlet for *Poly Role Models*. I was largely unfamiliar with this social-media network to start, but it soon became apparent that it had the right format, shareability, and audience for my needs.

With each weekly post to *Poly Role Models,* I update my presence on *Twitter* and *Facebook* to reflect the new information. If my work for the blog takes me away from home, I often take pictures with my cell phone, which I post to *Instagram.* These are all resources that I didn't need to spend additional money for, in connection to their use for the blog. These are all resources that give me immediate worldwide broadcast range.

It's very important to note that we are currently at an unprecedented point in human history as far as connectivity with the world around us. Things that have become basic necessities, like smartphones, computer access, and the Internet, have given people a massive platform that's theirs for the taking. There are free applications for recording video and sound. There is free software for the creation of text or graphic media.

Most importantly, there are free outlets to be able to share everything you make with the world around you.

Resources are often limited, and there will never be a universal solution around that, but in many cases it's still possible to take what you have and make it what you want.

CREATING AROUND TOKENISM...

Depending on what you're creating, working your way around tokenism can a bit dicey. As stated earlier, tokenism is about making halfhearted efforts to create the illusion of inclusivity. Since tokenism so frequently occurs when the people in charge all come from the same perspective, if you are working as an individual there's really only one possible perspective being represented. Even in writing this book, I'm speaking about people of color but my perspective is that of a lone black man. There's only so much that I will or would be able to see, on my own.

To counteract my own limited viewpoint, I've done my best to reach out to people with different interpretations than my own. Whether in the stories I've shared, or the information I've gathered, my voice is not the only one represented here. But the work I've done has always been intended as more of a conversation, and less of a lecture.

Sometimes, in conversation, you've got to let other people take the floor in order to explore new, and possibly better, ideas.

Have you ever seen *Mad Max: Fury Road*? It's pretty awesome! It was nominated for 10 Academy Awards, and managed to win six of them. It was easily my favorite movie of 2015. Aside from being an incredibly tense, and creatively shot action movie, set in the most-beautifully stylized wasteland imaginable, the movie gained pretty high praise for its feminist themes and the overall way its female characters were depicted.

Although the name of the movie implies that Mad Max is the focus, the film really revolves around the motivations of Imperator Furiosa (played by Charlize Theron) and The Brides; five women under Furiosa's care. Without giving too much away, because you seriously should just own a copy of this film, the women of *Fury Road* are all depicted as capable within the scope of their characters. As a hardened soldier, Furiosa is often shown as more capable of a fighter than Mad Max. Even though The Brides are technically damsels who are in distress, they don't fall into the stereotype. No one is waiting for a big, strong man to come and save them. Max is no exception. These women fit into the narrative and the harsh world the film is based in, without any exaggeration of their strengths or weakness.

Strangely, this is a task in which most movies fail.

Part of why *this* movie succeeded, was the inclusion of Eve Ensler as a consultant. Ensler is a feminist actor, performer, and playwright who is best known for her play *The Vagina Monologues*. Her contribution to the film was to make sure that the female characterizations felt more honest. Having spent more than two decades traveling the world, and working to end violence against women, Ensler had a wealth of knowledge and lived experience to offer the actors that the writers, the producers, and the director — all men — just didn't have access to.

The idea of men bringing in women to get the women in their stories right sounds simple. But it's still too rare in reality. Case in point, the comic books based on *Mad Max: Fury Road*. These books were created by the same male writing staff of the movie, but did not have Eve Ensler as a consultant. They received heavy criticism for the way the exact same female characters were handled. The motivations, solidarity, and capability that made them strong and fantastic in the film, were all stripped from them in the comic books. Graphic depictions of sexual assault were used in place of the film's subtle implications.

It was as if the writers had used up their limited supply of nuance on the film's script and only had bucketfuls of played-out tropes left for the comics. It's a pretty stark example of what happens when you let people tell their own stories…and when you don't.

About two months after *Poly Role Models* took off, I received a message from one of the readers. This reader asked me if any of the contributors to my blog had disabilities or were on the autism spectrum. I didn't know and, before the inclusion of the question that focused on self-identities, I wasn't specifically asking. While the blog was about showcasing diversity, I had yet to add that designated place to do so.

It would've been really easy to blow off the question. I could've said that the neurodiverse crowd simply hadn't shown up. Or I could've cited my own limited knowledge of such disabilities as the reason for a lack of diversity, and that likely would've ended the conversation. It also would have ended my blog's premise of being a resource devoted to offering a platform for the underrepresented. Instead, I took a different tack. I posted the reader's question publicly and asked for help.

Soon after I did this, I received messages from other readers who had more experience with, and knowledge of, disabilities than I had. Through this influx of new information, I was able to reach out to a polyamorous blogger with Asperger's syndrome. I got some letter-writing assistance from a partner who has some familiarity with Asperger's, and I communicated the needs of the blog, and let this blogger do their thing.

What I received from this blogger, was one of the most personal and informative entries in the blog's history. Not only was the profile amazing, the author immediately followed up its publishing with a second entry that drove even deeper into the intersection of autism and polyamory. Had the self-identities questions been available then, the follow-up might not have been needed. Instead, that follow-up became the signpost that such a question was necessary. It would be added to the submission form the very next week.

So, what happened in this situation, is that I gave up control of my platform, and opened it up to ideas outside of my own. As far as representation goes, the goals of my blog are clear, but I understand that I don't have the tools to manage them. Not completely and not by myself. Had I kept my hands on the steering wheel, this bit of magic would never have occurred. Furthermore, I'd have lost the idea that my platform was welcoming to neurodiverse people or people with disabilities.

I didn't want to be the kind of privileged person who tells oppressed people what their version of diversity should look like. It's the reason why I readily accept nominations for blog contributors. Everyone can have a hand in the creative process, in as much as it pertains to them. So, instead of trying to control the narrative, the pen was passed to those with lived experience to express themselves in the way that felt most authentic to them. In response, *Poly Role Models* became a more honest and welcoming resource, especially with the newly inspired question.

Since then, several contributors to the blog have openly discussed the ways in which their mental or physical disabilities, or illnesses, have affected the way they practice their polyamory.

As far as your own creations, you can still avoid tokenization by seeking additional opinions. This doesn't have to mean completely giving away control of your creative process. It could simply mean making your creative process more inclusive, to avoid writing people as stereotypes. Join an artists' collective or a writers' circle, or any manner of group dedicated to sharing and creating and offering opinions. If a group doesn't exist, you can form one of your own, locally or online.

Extend your perspective to people, and receive their perspective in return. Anything to avoid further marginalizing groups that you wish to include. If it means that your work is relatable and genuine to others beyond yourself, it could be worth it.

CREATING AROUND OTHERING...

As I mentioned before, "othering" has to do with having your differences used to keep you at arm's length, and the choice to engage organically being taken out of your hands. In the instances where I've felt like I was being othered, I would much rather have been drawn into a conversation by a common thread. In the culture that we're trying to put forward, that common thread is ethical non-monogamy.

Now, obviously everyone has to speak their own truth. First and foremost, we all should try to create whatever we feel is the most honest and meaningful to ourselves. But, as this is a book about challenging the way polyamory is represented, I mean to encourage that type of culture shift in the created works this book may inspire. If we're centering our discussion around ethical non-monogamy, that is a focus that can bring all interested people together. Once at the table, though, each creator can choose to share their personal observations...whether individualized, or as part of a shared cultural experience.

The most important part here is the ability to opt in or opt out of this part of the dialogue, at will. Othering occurs when someone else puts that spotlight on you without your consent. If you are creating your own material, the spotlight is yours to control. You can decide to write about the blurred lines between swinging and polyamory, and leave it at that. If you choose to approach the topic by invoking your own personal insight, as a person of color, that is 100% up to you. Even if you don't want to use that perspective, just being a person of color who is writing about that concept of ethical non-monogamy will be meaningful to the readership.

Our visibility is valuable unto itself.

As it pertains to my own work, the interview series serves the dual-function of visibility and self-motivated identification. The photos of each featured guest of *Poly Role Models* provide an immediate visual indicator that polyamory can look more than one way…for anyone who might question whether it can.

The eighth question of the interview is about which self-identities are important to the respondent, and how that self-identity may impact their polyamory. This question is optional. Readers of my blog show up to see how a variety of people relate to polyamory. Whether that includes a specific breakdown of how race factors in for a particular contributor is left completely at the discretion of that contributor. If they feel it's relevant, they will let us know. No othering applicable.

CREATING AROUND FETISHIZATION…

This one is actually sort of easy. Sharing your stories and experiences automatically works against fetishization without the effort of even trying to. Fetishization at its root is about simplification. The perpetrator of fetishization eroticizes a person as an object, a collection of stereotypes, clichés, and tropes to put in a box and categorize. Any manner of media that envisions a marginalized person as a full-fledged human being naturally fights that concept.

While someone may see me as "the black guy," my own writing describes me as a polyamorous, "have passport will travel," sports-loving, geekboy, movie buff, marathon runner, who's raising a pair of kids into the viewpoints of social justice and intersectional feminism.

I'm black, too, though.

You're gonna have to find a way to date, love, or sleep with me based on something other than my race. There's an awful lot to choose from.

Poly Role Models approaches self-identities in a way that isn't shallow or even based on an externalized viewpoint. Each contributor is asked to select which parts of themselves are most important, and to speak on those parts introspectively. If two contributors write about the same identity, they will almost doubtlessly approach it from two separate angles. Whether there are similarities or not, the uniqueness of the writers will create a uniqueness in the writing. Both will expand outside of the stereotype.

Anything you choose to create will have the same effect. Our lives aren't tropes. Our people are not a monolith. We are everybody and everything. Like Samuel L. Jackson says in *Unbreakable*, "Real life doesn't fit inside little boxes that were drawn for it."

Go out and prove it. To yourself and to everyone else!

TOO LONG / DIDN'T READ

I know this was a lot to take in. The thing to remember is that, in this process, we're all works in progress. If you're looking for the finish line, you won't find it. Creating inclusive communities isn't a game you can just win before walking off the field. It's not the Stanley Cup. Your name won't be etched on your success forever.

Not unless you keep at it.

That's gotta be enough.

Putting together a platform in which polyamorous people come to love and find safety, fellowship, and fulfillment has to be its own reward.

You picked up this book, though. So I have to believe that you already understand this. I have to believe that your goal was to give people of color a comfortable place within a structure you're responsible for, whether that be a group, a relationship, or just an individual interaction.

If your goal was to get a badge of honor, you're gonna have a harder time than you'd like. To this end, the hardest part of any of these measures is being able to withstand the discomfort of the conversation itself. The ability to listen in the face of that discomfort, and not become defensive is a virtue.

I could get angry and standoffish every time I hear women complain about their oppression at the hands of men…sometimes I even do. None of us are perfect, in that regard. But it's counterproductive.

Making changes, to yourself and the world around you, is never easy. If my intent is to put good into this world, it makes more sense to get introspective. How much does my behavior factor directly into the pain others feel? What can I do to reduce that? It helps to remember that as much as it hurts me to hear, it probably hurts them more to say and feel.

So, take the time to listen, self-examine, and act. None of this was written to be malicious, in the same way that I don't assume malice when I find myself uncomfortable in a polyamorous space. But just because discomfort felt by people of color might be unintentional, doesn't mean that a continued lack of intent is acceptable. Once you're aware of the struggle, we all need to find the room to be better and do better.

This book was all about making people aware.

Now that you're more aware, take this discussion with you. Include and project the voices of underrepresented people in the spaces where their access is limited. Go love, and build, and restore, and speak, and engage, and create. Go be better and do better.

Thank you...

ENDNOTES

Page 3 Zone of Proximal Development

Berk, L and Winsler, A. (1995). "Vygotsky: His Life and Works" and "Vygotsky's Approach To Development." In *Scaffolding Children's Learning: Vygotsky and Early Childhood Learning*. National Association for Education Of Young Children. p. 24

Page 9 Louis Brandeis quotation

Louis D. Brandeis Legacy Fund for Social Justice. (n.d.). Retrieved February 23, 2017, from http://www.brandeis.edu/legacyfund/bio.html

Page 23 Louis C.K. sketch

Jost, C. (Writer), Klein, R. (Writer) & King, D.R. (Director). (2015). Louis C.K./Rhianna [Television series episode]. In L. Michaels (Executive producer), *Saturday Night Live*. New York, NY: NBC Broadcasting.

Page 26 Matthew Heimbach

Towson University Student Proposes To Start A White Student Union On Campus. (n.d.). Retrieved February 23, 2017, from http://baltimore.cbslocal.com/2012/09/07/towson-university-student-proposes-to-start-a-white-student-union-on-campus/

Page 27 Towson student demographics

Student Enrollment Data. (n.d.). Retrieved February 23, 2017, from http://www.towson.edu/provost/institutionalresearch/enrollment.html

Page 31 Justin Trudeau quote

CBC News. (2015, November 04). Justin Trudeau speaks following swearing-in at Rideau Hall. [Video File]. Retrieved from https://www.youtube.com/watch?v=5Jfgsfp0ZdM.

Page 40 Nicki Minaj tweet

Minaj, N. (2015, July 21). Twitter/@NICKIMINAJ

Page 41

Taylor Swift tweet

Swift, T. (2015, July 21). Twitter/@taylorswift13

Nicki Minaj fan tweet

B. (2015, July 21). Twitter/@itsbereniced

Page 43 Defintion of "intersectionality"

Crenshaw, K. (1991, 07). "Mapping the Margins: Intersectionality,
      Identity Politics, and Violence Against Women Of Color."
      Stanford Law Review, 43(6), 1241. doi:10.2307/1229039

Page 44 Books on polyamory

Easton, D., & Hardy, J. W. (2009). *The Ethical Slut: A
      Practical Guide to Polyamory, Open Relations and
      Other Adventures*. Berkeley, CA: Celestial Art.

Veaux, F., & Rickert, E. (2014). *More Than Two: A Practical Guide
      To Ethical Polyamory*. Portland, OR: Thorntree Press.

Sheff, E. (2015). *The Polyamorists Next Door: Inside Multiple-Partner
      Relationships and Families*. Lanham: Rowman & Littlefield.

Block, J. (2009). *Open: Love, Sex, and Life In an
      Open Marriage*. Berkeley, CA: Seal Press.

Ryan, C., & Jethá, C. (2011). *Sex At Dawn: The Prehistoric Origins Of
      Modern Sexuality*. Carlton North, Vic.: Scribe Publications.

Page 45 Books on polyamory

Anapol, D. M. (2011). *Polyamory In the Twenty-First Century: Love and
      Intimacy With Multiple Partners*. Lanham, Md.: Rowman & Littlefield.

Minx, C. (2014). *Eight Things I Wish I'd Known About Polyamory:
      Before I Tried It and Frakked It Up*. Seattle, WA: Do The Work.

Taormino, T. (2008). *Opening Up: A Guide To Creating and
      Sustaining Open Relationships*. San Francisco, CA: Cleis Press.

Page 46 Steph Guthrie tweet

Guthrie, S. (2013, March 8). Twitter/@amirightfolks

Page 47   "Poly" as an abbreviation for "Polynesian"

Manduley, Aida. "Stop Saying 'Poly' When You Mean 'Polyamorous.'" (2015, September 1). Retrieved September 11, 2017, from http://aidamanduley. com/2015/09/01/stop-saying-poly-when-you-mean-polyamorous/

Stone, Lily. "Poly Means Polynesian, Not Polyamorous." (2016, January 20). Retrieved February 23, 2017, from https://medium.com/guerrilla-feminism/ poly-means-polynesian-not-polyamorous-by-lily-stone-2e401e5338f6

Page 51   Studies on pain and racial bias

Forgiarini, M., Gallucci, M., & Maravita, A. (2011). "Racism and the Empathy for Pain on Our Skin." *Frontiers in Psychology, 2.* doi:10.3389/fpsyg.2011.00108

Hoffman, K. M., Trawalter, S., Axt, J. R., & Oliver, M. N. (2016, 04). "Racial Bias In Pain Assessment and Treatment Recommendations, and False Beliefs About Biological Differences Between Blacks and Whites." *Proceedings Of the National Academy Of Sciences, 113*(16), 4296–4301. doi:10.1073/pnas.1516047113

Todd, K. H., Deaton, C., D'Adamo, A. P., & Goe, L. (2000, 01). "Ethnicity and Analgesic Practice." *Annals of Emergency Medicine 35*(1), 11–16. doi:10.1016/s0196-0644(00)70099-0

Page 52   Definition of "othering"

Oxford Living Dictionary.com (2017). The Oxford University Press. Retrieved June 27, 2017, from https:// en.oxforddictionaries.com/definition/other

Page 58
Emma Tessler quote

Establishment, T. (2015, October 30). "Yes, Your Dating Preferences Are Probably Racist." Retrieved February 27, 2017, from https://theestablishment.co/yes-your-dating-preferenc-es-are-probably-racist-e58ae2fd625d#.tiwdk57se

Christian Rudder book

Rudder, C. (2015). *Dataclysm: Who We Are (When We Think No One's Looking).* London: Fourth Estate.

Page 59 Study on race and dating preferences

Liu, J. H., Campbell, S. M., & Condie, H. (1995, 01). "Ethnocentrism
    In Dating Preferences For an American Sample: The
    Ingroup Bias In Cocial Context." *European Journal of Social
    Psychology, 25*(1), 95–115. doi:10.1002/ejsp.2420250108

Page 63 Mere exposure effect

Zajonc, R. B. (1968). "Attitudinal Effects Of Mere Exposure." *Journal of
    Personality and Social Psychology, 9*(2, Pt.2), 1–27. doi:10.1037/h0025848
Zebrowitz, L. A., White, B., & Wieneke, K. (2008, 06). "Mere
    Exposure and Racial Prejudice: Exposure To Other-Race
    Faces Increases Liking For Strangers Of That Race." *Social
    Cognition, 26*(3), 259-275. doi:10.1521/soco.2008.26.3.259

Page 68 Carrie Jenkins article

Establishment, T. (2016, July 27). "Dear Media: Polyamory Is Not All About
    Sex." Retrieved February 27, 2017, from https://theestablishment.co/
    dear-media-polyamory-is-not-all-about-sex-6216830b9d39#.98i5h4h2v

Page 71 WOCSHN

WOCSHN – Women of Color Sexual Health Network. (n.d.).
    Retrieved February 27, 2017, from http://www.wocshn.org/

Page 73 Interview with Aisha Tyler

Avery, K. (Writer), Bell, W.K. (Writer) & Perota, J. (Director). (2013).
    Show 21 [Television series episode]. In C. Rock (Executive producer),
    Totally Biased with W. Kamau Bell. New York, NY: Comedy Central.

Page 76

Polyamory: Married and Dating

Garcia, N. (Writer), Garcia, N. (Director). (2012). In G. Berman (Executive
    producer), *Polyamory: Married & Dating*. New York, NY: Showtime.

Emily Yoshida article

Yoshida, E. (2012, July 20). "Things I Learned From Showtime's
    Polyamory: Married and Dating." Retrieved February 27,
    2017, from http://grantland.com/hollywood-prospectus/
    things-i-learned-from-showtimes-polyamory-married-and-dating/

Page 78 *Compersion* **YouTube series**

Enchant TV. (n.d.). Retrieved February 27, 2017, from https://www.
youtube.com/channel/UC6j_NECgCP7cKji86GjoAMg

Page 83 *The New York Times Magazine* **article**

Dominus, S. (2017, May 11). "Is an Open Marriage a Happier
Marriage?" *The New York Times Magazine.* Retrieved
from https://www.nytimes.com/2017/05/11/magazine/
is-an-open-marriage-a-happier-marriage.html

Page 84 **Dale Spender research**

Spender, D., Sarah, E., & Mahony, P. (1980). *Learning to Lose:
Sexism and Education.* London: The Women's Press.

Page 87 **Responses to** *The New York Times Magazine* **article**

Johnson, R. B. (28 May, 2017). "The Times Piece About Open Marriages
Doesn't Represent My Experience." Retrieved from http://www.
huffingtonpost.com/entry/how-representation-worksordoesnt_
us_59179e37e4b00ccaae9ea39d?ncid=engmodushpmg00000003

Polyamory Weekly (29 May 2018). "That NYT Magazine
Article On Poly." Retrieved from http://polyweekly.
com/518-nyt-magazine-article-polyamory/

Page 88 *Tropes vs. Women in Video Games*

Ms. Male Character – Tropes vs. Women. (2016, August 25).
Retrieved February 27, 2017, from https://feministfrequency.
com/video/ms-male-character-tropes-vs-women/

Page 90 **Definition of "stereotype"**

Oxford Living Dictionary.com (2017). The Oxford
University Press. Retrieved June 27, 2017, from https://
en.oxforddictionaries.com/definition/stereotype

Page 95 **Bernie Sanders speech**

Sanders, Bernie. It's Very Expensive To Be Poor. (2015,
December 26). Retrieved February 27, 2017, from https://
www.youtube.com/watch?v=3CuzbI4e7Pk

Page 103 Jamie Johnson

The Art and Craft of Storytelling. (n.d.). Retrieved February 27, 2017, from https://themoth.org/storytellers/jamie-johnson

Page 112 Sexual assault statistics

Statistics. (n.d.). Retrieved February 27, 2017, from https://www.rainn.org/statistics

Page 118

Orange Is the New Black **episode**

Kohan, J. (Writer), McCarthy, A. (Director). (2016). "Work That Body For Me" [Television series episode] In J. Kohan (Executive producer), *Orange is the New Black*. Los Gatos, CA: Netflix.

Orange Is the New Black **writing staff**

Aran, I. (n.d.). Go Ahead, Guess How Many Black Writers Work on *Orange Is the New Black*. Retrieved February 27, 2017, from http://fusion.net/story/317498/oitnb-writers-room/

Page 141

Humans of New York

Humans of New York. (n.d.). Retrieved February 27, 2017, from http://www.humansofnewyork.com/

Girl on Guy

Tyler, A. (Host). (2011). *Girl on Guy* [Audio podcast]. Retrieved from http://www.girlonguy.net.

Self-Inflicted Wounds

Tyler, A. (2013). *Self-inflicted Wounds: Heartwarming Tales Of Epic Humiliation*. New York: It Books, an Imprint of HarperCollins.

Page 150 Samuel L. Jackson quote

Barber, G. (Producer), & Shyamalan, M.N. (Director). (2000). *Unbreakable* [Motion picture]. USA: Touchstone Pictures.

INDEX

ALSO FROM THORNAPPLE PRESS

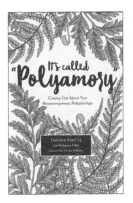

It's Called "Polyamory": Coming Out About Your Nonmonogamous Relationships

Tamara Pincus and Rebecca Hiles
With a foreword by Kendra Holliday

"Doing poly, holding poly space in the world, is hard work, often thankless. Thanks to this wonderful resource, it's now a lot easier."
   —Loraine Hutchins, co-editor, *Bi Any Other Name: Bisexual People Speak Out*

Playing Fair: A Guide to Nonmonogamy for Men Into Women

Pepper Mint

"Playing Fair is a brilliant road map for a more conscientious approach to ethical nonmonogamy."
   —from the foreword by Kevin A. Patterson

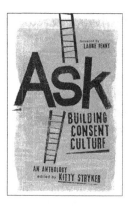

Ask: Building Consent Culture

Edited by Kitty Stryker
With a foreword by Laurie Penny
and an afterword by Carol Queen

*"There are certain conversations that deepen
how you think; positively impact how you
act; expand your view and understanding
of the world, and forever alter how you
approach it. This book is full of them. Make
room for it - then spread the word."*
   —Alix Fox, journalist, sex educator and ambas-
     sador for the Brook sexual wellbeing charity

When Someone You Love Is Polyamorous: Understanding Poly People and Relationships

Dr. Elisabeth Sheff

*An essential guidebook for family and
friends of polyamorous people.*